Christine McFadden was a gra~~~ ~~~
her passionate interest in foo~ ~~~
sufficiently strong for her to in~ ~~~
a degree in Home Economics. ~~~ ~~~ ~~~ first class
honours.

She now works as a freelance cookery writer and editor,
writing cookery books as well as articles about food and
nutrition for various consumer magazines.

Christine is an enthusiastic herb and vegetable gardener and
enjoys growing unusual plants. Her love of colourful, lively
ingredients is reflected in her recipes. She lives in Bath with her
husband, son and large cat, Woodstock.

HEALTHY MAIN MEAL SALADS

CHRISTINE McFADDEN

Photographs by Don Last

Little, Brown and Company
BOSTON NEW YORK TORONTO LONDON

A LITTLE, BROWN BOOK

First published in the United Kingdom
by Little, Brown and Company (UK) in 1995

Text copyright © 1995 Christine McFadden
Photographs © 1995 Don Last

A CIP catalogue for this book is available
from the British Library

ISBN 0 356 21100 2

Typeset by Solidus (Bristol) Limited
Printed and bound in Great Britain by
Clays Ltd, St. Ives plc

Little, Brown and Company (UK)
Brettenham House
Lancaster Place
London WC2E 7EN

Contents

Acknowledgements

I would like to thank my husband, Ed, for uncomplainingly eating salads for three months. Many thanks also to Veronica Sperling for her invaluable help in testing the recipes.

Introduction

Oh, green and glorious! Oh, herbaceous treat!
T'would tempt the dying anchorite to eat;
Back to the world he'd turn his fleeting soul,
And plunge his fingers in the salad bowl!
Serenely full, the epicure would say,
'Fate cannot harm me, I have dined today.'

'Recipe for a Salad', Selected Letters,
Sydney Smith 1771–1845

Many people think that a good meal has to be a hot one, but as Sydney Smith implies, it's simply not true. By combining an exciting range of the foods essential for a balanced diet, you can make mouthwatering, gutsy main meal salads which are the answer to today's healthy eating message. Lunches and evening meals become an enjoyable process of putting together ready-cooked or raw ingredients, while slaving over a hot stove becomes a thing of the past.

We all like to eat well, but these days few of us have the time, or perhaps the inclination, to spend long hours in the kitchen. The joy of main meal salads is that most of them are quick and easy to put together. All you need are a few salad greens, some good quality fragrant oils and vinegars, and the ability to see whatever food you happen to have on hand in terms of a salad. Some of the recipes take a little longer to prepare, but much of the work can be done ahead of time.

What makes a salad? Almost anything can become a salad – not just lettuce leaves, tomatoes and cucumber, but vegetables, grains, pulses, meat, poultry, fish, bread, eggs and cheese – hot, warm or cold. But what really differentiates a salad from other dishes is the dressing and the touch of acidity it provides – be it vinegar, lemon juice, yogurt or soured cream.

Once you get in the salad habit, you'll find your fridge and storecupboard always have the makings of a main meal salad – crisp salad leaves, fresh herbs, leftover waxy potatoes, a pot of creamy yogurt, bits of crispy bacon, cold-cuts, ready-made hummus, cooked rice or pulses, pasta, olives, cheeses and sun-dried tomatoes.

Visually appealing and full of sensational textures and flavours, the salads in this book are guaranteed to satisfy the most committed carnivore and vegetarian alike. Many of the recipes are for composed salads, in which the components are arranged attractively on individual plates or in a serving dish, rather than being tossed together in a bowl. Some of the recipes show you how to put several small servings of different salads on one plate. They are infinitely flexible – you can add or subtract components to suit your appetite, mood, or nutritional requirements.

Experimenting is part of the fun of cooking, and I hope the recipes will inspire you to create your own exciting main meal salads.

EASY AND ENJOYABLE HEALTHY EATING

The key to good health is a balanced diet – that is eating a wide variety of foods, and at the same time cutting down on fat and increasing fibre intake.

An easy way to look at your diet is to split it into three groups:

★ Vegetables, salads and fruit
★ Bread, potatoes and cereals
★ Meat, poultry, fish and dairy foods

You'll see that the main meal salads in this book use a good variety of foods from all three groups, so if you eat them on a regular basis you'll be putting the experts' advice into practice and eating a balanced diet.

Our bodies need five categories of nutrients in order to function properly: protein, carbohydrate, fat, vitamins and minerals. We also need fibre, which we get from various foods in the different categories.

The nutrients in food do not work in isolation. They form a tightly knit team which supplies the body's entire needs. Fortunately, most foods are a complex mixture of several nutrients. So creating main meal salads, using components from all three food groups, provides a rich source of all the essential nutrients.

PROTEIN

Protein provides amino acids which are vital for the growth, repair and maintenance of the body. If you are a vegetarian, it is particularly important to eat a wide range of grains, pulses, nuts and seeds in order to get adequate protein. However, the proteins in these foods are deficient in one or more of the essential amino acids which make up 'complete' protein, found in meat, fish, eggs and dairy foods. But by eating two types of plant proteins together, such as cereal with beans, or nuts with cereals etc, the amino acids of one protein will compensate for those missing in another.

Good examples of protein combining are adding nuts to a rice salad, and serving bread or tortillas with bean salads. Another tip is to include small amounts of dairy foods, eg a slice of cheese or a yogurt dressing, in grain or pulse-based salads.

Good sources:
Meat, poultry, fish, seafood, cheese, eggs, yogurt, cream, tofu, beans, grains, lentils, chick-peas, nuts, seeds, sea vegetables, peas, cauliflower, broccoli, garlic, horseradish.

CARBOHYDRATE

Carbohydrate provides us with the fuel to produce the energy which keeps our bodies going. We get part of that fuel from the complex sugars, starches and cellulose (fibre) found in carbohydrate-rich foods such as grains, pulses, vegetables and fruits. Current nutritional guidelines recommend that we increase the amount of carbohydrate in the diet to supply 70 per cent of our energy needs. For most of us, that means doubling our intake.

Good sources:
Root vegetables, grains, rice, pasta, nuts, beans, chick-peas, lentils, peas, garlic, sweetcorn, dried apricots, grapes, bananas, pears.

FAT

Although you should be careful about the amount of fat you eat, it is an important part of a healthy diet. Fats and oils provide us with energy in a more concentrated form than carbohydrate, and they also provide warmth, essential nutrients and meal satisfaction. They improve the palatability of food.

The World Health Organisation recommends that fat should provide no more than 30 per cent of our energy needs. Most of us in the UK eat almost three times this amount, so we all need to cut down. You can do this by using low-fat dairy products, and lean cuts of meat and poultry.

Oils are obviously a major source of fat in salads, but unlike animal fats they are low in cholesterol and rich in mono-unsaturated fatty acids which do not clog your arteries.

Good sources:
Meat, poultry, oily fish, cream, cheese, yogurt, eggs, nuts, seeds, avocados, olives.

FIBRE

Dietary fibre is a form of carbohydrate found in the structural material which makes up the roots, stems, leaves, seeds and fruits of plants. It reduces the risk of bowel cancer, heart disease, obesity and diabetes. It also stimulates the digestive system, helps prevent constipation, and makes us feel full, therefore reducing calorie intake.

Good sources:
Root vegetables, green vegetables, sea vegetables, whole grains, pasta, beans, dried apricots, guavas.

CALCIUM

In addition to strengthening the bones, calcium is essential for muscle contraction, including the heart muscle, for nerve function, enzyme activity and for clotting of the blood.

Too little calcium in the diet results in stunted growth and rickets in young children, and osteoporosis (loss of bone tissue) in post-menopausal women.

Good sources:
Parmesan cheese, Edam, Cheddar, anchovies, yogurt, almonds, hazelnuts, Brazil nuts, pine nuts, sesame seeds, tofu, chick-peas, dried apricots, lemons, oranges, olives, sesame oil, cumin, coriander seeds, sea vegetables, tuna fish, mangetout, beetroot, broccoli, celeriac, kale, horseradish, parsnips, garlic, onions.

MAGNESIUM

Magnesium is an essential constituent of our body cells. It activates energy-releasing enzymes and helps the body make proteins.

Good sources:
Meat, poultry, cream, yogurt, cheese, eggs, bread, grains, nuts, seeds, pulses, dried fruit, sea vegetables, root vegetables, ginger, garlic.

IRON

Iron is involved in the production of red blood cells, the functioning of several enzymes and in transporting oxygen around the body. A deficiency results in anaemia, the symptoms of which include tiredness, breathlessness, pale skin and irritability.

Good sources:
Red meat, eggs, sea vegetables, basil, cumin seeds, parsley, cashew nuts, sesame seeds, dried apricots, haricot beans, kidney beans, spinach, watercress, anchovies, mussels.

ZINC

Zinc is one of the most versatile of minerals. It regulates the activities of hundreds of enzymes, and is involved in the metabolism of proteins, carbohydrate, energy and genetic material within the cells. It is essential for growth, especially of the foetus during pregnancy, for the formation of bone tissue, the development of reproductive organs, the healing of wounds and for maintaining a healthy immune system. It is also thought to be helpful in preventing and shortening colds.

Good sources:
Sea vegetables, buckwheat, anchovies, scallops, sardines, crab, beef, liver, aduki beans, lentils, garlic, egg yolk, Brazil nuts, cashew nuts, pine nuts, sesame seeds, Parmesan cheese, Stilton, Edam.

POTASSIUM

Potassium is needed for the normal functioning of the nerves and muscles, and is involved in enzyme activity and protein metabolism. It works in a complementary way to sodium (salt) in the functioning of cells and in the concentration and balance of fluids within the cells. Most of us have too much sodium in our diet and too little potassium.

Good sources:
Cheese, yogurt, citrus fruit, meat, poultry, fish, potatoes, beans, lentils, green vegetables, beetroot, chillies, garlic, nuts, seeds.

SELENIUM

There is a great deal of controversy around selenium. Positive claims state that it protects our cells against damage from harmful oxidation, protects against heart disease and stroke, inhibits cancer, strengthens the immune system, delays ageing and protects against toxic substances such as heavy metals, alcohol and cigarette smoke. On the other hand, some experts believe that selenium is carcinogenic, highly toxic, and cannot be used by the body when taken with vitamin C.

Good sources:
Brazil nuts, sunflower seeds, cashew nuts, walnuts, lentils, wholemeal bread, sardines, tuna, mussels, shrimps, rabbit, pork.

VITAMIN A (CAROTENE AND RETINOL)

Vitamin A is essential for vision in dim light, and for the maintenance of healthy skin and mucous membranes.

Retinol is the chemical name for vitamin A and is found only in animal foods. Milk and some plants contain carotenes which are converted in the body to vitamin A.

Good sources:
Cream, yogurt, hard cheeses, eggs, liver, salmon, herring, sardines, basil, coriander, parsley, dried apricots, guava, papaya, sea vegetables, mangetout, sweet potatoes, broccoli, carrots, kale, leeks, lettuce, chillies, red peppers, spinach, tomatoes, watercress, pistachio nuts, sunflower seeds.

B VITAMINS

The B group of vitamins are composed of eight actual vitamins, including folate, and several vitamin-like compounds. They have a huge influence on our health. They are mainly involved with the release of energy from food within the body. They are required for the functioning of the immune system, the digestive system, the heart and muscles and for the production of new blood cells. Some of the B vitamins have anti-oxidant properties.

Good sources:
Meat, poultry, eggs, fish, cheese, pulses, spinach, cauliflower, dried apricots, wholemeal bread, cabbage, carrots, potatoes, brown rice, nuts, seeds.

VITAMIN C

Vitamin C is essential for good health. It increases iron absorption, helps with the formation of bones, teeth and tissues, it speeds the healing of wounds, helps keep the skin elastic and improves resistance to infection, high blood pressure, arteriosclerosis and cancer. Our bodies cannot make it themselves so have to get it from food. It is a very unstable vitamin and is easily destroyed by heat and oxidation.

Good sources:
Watercress, potatoes, broad beans, mangetout, broccoli, cabbage, cauliflower, horseradish, kohlrabi, chillies, red peppers, grapefruit, guava, oranges, lemons, papaya, coriander.

VITAMIN D

The main function of vitamin D is to maintain adequate calcium levels in the blood. Without it, the body cannot absorb calcium. Vitamin D comes from two entirely different sources: it can be manufactured directly by the body in the skin by exposure to sunlight, or it can be supplied by food.

Good sources:
Eggs, liver, cream, yogurt, cheese, oily fish.

VITAMIN E

Vitamin E is essential for the protection of the billions of cells which make up our bodies. Together with vitamins A and C, it is known as an anti-oxidant. This means it neutralises highly reactive forms of oxygen and substances known as free radicals which attack the cells. Vitamin E is also involved in red blood cell formation.

Good sources:
Vegetable oils, nuts and nut oils, seeds, cream, Parmesan cheese, Cheddar, parsley, bacon, avocados, olives, chick-peas, carrots, parsnips, red peppers, spinach, tomatoes, watercress, sweetcorn.

1

Vegetable and Leaf Salads

This chapter features salads made with raw or cooked vegetables and the more robust salad leaves, such as young spinach, rocket, watercress, endive and radicchio. Toasted nuts and seeds, good quality bread and zesty dressings complete the picture.

Cooked vegetables are roasted or grilled to bring out the full flavour; or otherwise briefly steamed or parboiled to tenderise them, and then rinsed under cold running water to stop the cooking. Prepared this way, the vegetables not only retain more nutrients, but they remain crunchy and brightly coloured – essential features of a successful salad.

Served alone, these salads make a lightish main meal. Add a serving of cooked grains, a slice of good cheese, or some salami, and you have the makings of a full-blown main meal.

ASPARAGUS, MUSHROOM AND FENNEL SALAD WITH HAZELNUTS

SERVES 2

Asparagus contains the anti-oxidant vitamins A, E and C, thought to protect against cancer. Blanching as quickly as possible retains maximum nutrients and keeps the asparagus crisp and green.

350 g/12 oz thin asparagus, trimmed
3 tbsp olive oil
100 g/4 oz assorted mushrooms, such as shiitake, chestnut, oyster,
ceps, cut into even-sized pieces
1 garlic clove, finely chopped
squeeze of lemon juice
2 tbsp chopped fresh tarragon
salt and freshly ground black pepper
1 handful each red oak lettuce and frisee, torn into
bite-sized pieces
½ fennel bulb, quartered, cored and thinly sliced
2 shallots, finely chopped
4 tbsp Hazelnut Vinaigrette (page 188)
40 g/1½ oz toasted hazelnuts, roughly chopped

Plunge the asparagus into boiling water for 2–3 minutes until just tender. Drain under cold running water and pat dry with paper towel. Cut off the tips and chop the stalks into 1 cm/½ inch pieces.

Heat the oil in a pan until very hot. Add the mushrooms and stir-fry for 2 minutes. Add the garlic, lemon juice, half the tarragon, and salt and pepper. Stir-fry for another minute. Leave to cool.

Arrange the salad leaves and fennel on a serving dish or individual plates. Add the asparagus stalks and mushrooms.

Whisk the shallots and remaining tarragon with the vinaigrette, then pour over the salad and toss to mix. Arrange the asparagus tips on top and sprinkle with the hazelnuts.

SPICY SPINACH FRITTATA WITH ROASTED PEPPER AND YOGURT SAUCE

SERVES 4–6

Normally made with whole eggs, this version of the frittata uses half the usual amount of egg yolks, which considerably reduces the cholesterol content. Leftovers will keep for several days in the fridge but allow to come to room temperature before serving.

250 g/9 oz young spinach
4 eggs (size 2)
4 egg whites
¼ tsp salt
freshly ground black pepper
40 g/1½ oz toasted pine nuts
2 tbsp sunflower oil
25 g/1 oz butter
4 spring onions, finely chopped
2 cm/¾ inch piece fresh ginger root, finely chopped
1 fresh green chilli, seeded and finely chopped
½ tsp ground turmeric
4 tomatoes, sliced
1 cos lettuce, torn into bite-sized pieces
4 tender celery stalks, sliced
small bunch of radishes, sliced
1 tbsp olive oil
Roasted Pepper and Yogurt Sauce (page 201), to serve

Remove the stems from the spinach and roughly chop the leaves. Beat the eggs and whites with the salt and pepper. Stir in the pine nuts.

Heat the oil and butter in a 24–25 cm/9 ½–10 inch non-stick frying pan. Gently fry the onions, ginger and chilli with the turmeric for a minute or two.

Stir in the spinach, cover and cook for about 5 minutes until just wilted. Raise the heat and stir-fry, uncovered, until the liquid has evaporated.

Add the egg mixture, stirring to evenly distribute the spinach. Cook over a medium-low heat for about 10 minutes until almost set. Slide the frittata onto a plate, cover with the pan, then invert it back into the pan. Briefly return to the heat to brown the second side.

Toss the tomatoes, lettuce, celery and radishes with the oil.

Cut the frittata into thin wedges and serve warm or at room temperature with roasted pepper and yogurt sauce and the salad.

SALAD OF ROASTED LEEKS, TOMATO AND OLIVES

SERVES 2

Serve the leeks slightly warm or at room temperature. You could add some of the Spicy Spinach Frittata (page 5), cut into thin wedges and tucked in amongst the lettuce and tomatoes.

6–8 small leeks, trimmed and left whole
3 tbsp extra virgin olive oil
coarse sea salt
2 tbsp chopped fresh mixed herbs, such as thyme, lovage, flat-leafed
parsley, chives, rosemary
½ tsp balsamic vinegar
coarsely ground black pepper
4 handfuls red oak lettuce
3 plum tomatoes, seeded and cut into segments
12 pitted black olives
Garlic Croutons (page 184)
2 hard-boiled eggs, chopped
4 radishes, halved lengthways

Pack the leeks in a shallow ovenproof dish just large enough to hold them in a single layer. Add the olive oil, turning the leeks until well coated. Sprinkle with coarse sea salt.

Roast in the top of a preheated oven at 250°C/500°F/gas 9 for 10 minutes. Turn and roast for another 10 minutes until beginning to blacken.

Remove from the oven, allow to cool a little, then cut crossways into 5 cm/2 inch pieces. Put in a small bowl and stir in the herbs. Sprinkle with the balsamic vinegar and a few grindings of black pepper. Add a little sea salt if necessary.

Toss the lettuce in a drop of oil – enough to barely coat the leaves – and arrange on individual plates or in a shallow serving dish. Pile the leeks in the middle. Scatter the tomatoes, olives and croutons around the edge.

Scatter the chopped eggs over the leeks and garnish with the radish slices.

ROASTED VEGETABLE SALAD

SERVES 3–4

A really colourful robust salad full of strong fruity flavours –
ideal for a summer buffet. Serve with plenty of warm ciabatta
bread to mop up the juices.

½ Oven-Dried Aubergine (page 177)
2 small Roasted Courgettes (page 180)
1 yellow Roasted Pepper (page 178)
1 escarole or cos lettuce
handful of rocket
2 hard-boiled eggs, quartered
8 cherry tomatoes, halved
4 oil-cured bottled artichokes, quartered
Parmesan shavings
torn basil leaves
1 tbsp snipped fresh chives
3 tbsp extra virgin olive oil
1 tbsp balsamic vinegar
salt and freshly ground black pepper

Cut the aubergine slices crossways into 2.5 cm/1 inch pieces,
the courgettes into 5 cm/2 inch pieces and the pepper into
matchstick strips.

Make a bed of escarole leaves and rocket on a large shallow
serving dish. Arrange the roasted vegetables, hard-boiled eggs,
tomatoes and artichokes on top. Scatter with Parmesan shavings and basil, and sprinkle the chives over the eggs.

Drizzle with the oil, then the vinegar and season to taste.
Serve at once.

CIABATTA SALAD

SERVES 2–3

A good way of using up ciabatta bread which is past its best.

4 × 2.5 cm / 1 inch slices ciabatta bread
5–6 tbsp extra virgin olive oil
2 cloves Roasted Garlic (page 183)
75 g / 3 oz green beans
finely grated zest of ½ lemon
juice of 1 lemon
salt and freshly ground black pepper
4 spring onions, green parts included, thinly sliced
½ green pepper, seeded and diced
8 cherry tomatoes, halved
1 tbsp chopped fresh flat-leafed parsley
1 tbsp chopped fresh mixed herbs, such as marjoram, thyme, basil
1 Little Gem or small cos lettuce, torn into bite-sized pieces
12 pitted black olives

Drizzle the bread on both sides with some of the olive oil and smear with the garlic. Bake in a preheated oven at 220°C/425°F/gas 7 for 10–15 minutes until golden and crisp. Cut into 1 cm/½ inch cubes.

Plunge the beans into plenty of boiling salted water for 3 minutes. Drain, then chop into 2 cm/¾ inch pieces.

Put the beans in a serving bowl while still warm, and toss with the lemon zest and juice, salt and pepper, and remaining oil. Add the onions, green pepper, tomatoes, parsley and herbs, and toss well.

When ready to serve, add the ciabatta, lettuce and olives. Check the seasoning and serve at once.

LEBANESE PITTA BREAD SALAD

SERVES 2–3

The bread makes this a substantial salad, but you could add some chopped hard-boiled egg or crumbled feta cheese for protein. It would also be good with diced grilled lamb or chicken, or Hummus with Lime (page 168), Cucumber and Yogurt (page 167), or Oven-Dried Tomatoes (page 157).

2 wholemeal pitta breads
juice of 1 lemon
4 tbsp extra virgin olive oil
½ cucumber
3 spring onions, green parts included, chopped
1 green pepper, seeded and chopped
2 plum tomatoes, seeded and chopped
1 tbsp chopped fresh flat-leafed parsley
1 tbsp chopped fresh coriander
½ tsp cumin seeds
salt and freshly ground black pepper

Toast the bread on both sides and then cut into 2 cm/¾ inch pieces. Put in a bowl and add the lemon juice and 2 tablespoons of the olive oil, tossing to coat. Leave to stand for 15 minutes.

Quarter the cucumber lengthways, remove the seeds, then chop into 2 cm/¾ inch chunks. Put in a salad bowl with the onions, pepper and tomatoes.

Add the parsley, coriander, cumin and remaining olive oil, and season to taste.

Stir in the bread, adding more lemon juice or oil if necessary. Serve at once.

MIDDLE EASTERN SALAD PLATTER

SERVES 2–3

A flexible salad based on a traditional meze, using a selection of delicious small salads. Use whatever's to hand. Green Bean, Lemon and Sesame Salad (page 163), Minted Ratatouille (page 166), Tomato and Cucumber Salsa (page 169) and Aubergine, Chilli and Sesame Dip (page 172) would all be good.

1 small cos lettuce, torn into bite-sized pieces
2 plum tomatoes, cut into segments
½ small red onion, thinly sliced
½ green pepper, seeded and thinly sliced
a few pitted black olives
2 tbsp chopped fresh flat-leafed parsley
salt and freshly ground black pepper
squeeze of lemon juice
3 tbsp extra virgin olive oil
175 g/6 oz cooked Puy lentils (about 75 g/3 oz dry weight)
Cucumber and Yogurt (page 167)
Hummus with Lime (page 168)
1 Oven-Dried Aubergine (page 177)

Put the lettuce, tomatoes, onion, green pepper, olives and half the parsley in a bowl, and toss with the seasoning, lemon juice and half the oil.

Mix the lentils with lemon juice to taste, add salt and pepper, and the remaining oil and parsley.

Divide the salad and the lentils between individual plates and add the cucumber and yogurt, hummus and aubergine.

BEETROOT, ORANGE AND ROCKET SALAD WITH PUMPKIN SEEDS

SERVES 2

Traditionally relegated to the boring British salad, beetroot takes on a new lease of life here. Peppery rocket, bitter chicory and juicy oranges counteract its sweetness, while the pumpkin seeds add crunch. The salad looks especially dramatic made with blood oranges. Beetroot is rich in potassium and folate. It also provides some calcium, iron, zinc and vitamin C.

4 small fresh beetroot, trimmed
3 tbsp chopped fresh parsley
Orange Vinaigrette (page 192)
salt and freshly ground black pepper
2 heads red chicory
4 handfuls trimmed rocket
2 hard-boiled eggs, sliced
2 oranges, peeled and thinly sliced
2 spring onions, quartered lengthways and cut into
2.5 cm/1 inch shreds
2 tbsp toasted pumpkin seeds
few drops of pumpkin seed oil

Wrap the beetroot loosely in foil and bake in a preheated oven at 180°C/350°F/gas 4 for 1 hour, until easily pierced with a skewer. Peel and slice thinly.

Mix the beetroot with the parsley and half the dressing. Season to taste and set aside.

Arrange the chicory leaves like a star around the edge of individual plates, with the rocket on top. Put the eggs in the centre, with overlapping beetroot and orange slices round the edge. Scatter the spring onions over the beetroot and oranges. Sprinkle the pumpkin seeds over the egg.

Drizzle with the remaining dressing and a few drops of pumpkin seed oil.

RED RED SALAD WITH GRILLED POLENTA AND ROCKET

SERVES 2–3

I often wonder why beetroot is the only root vegetable sold cooked when it's easy to cook yourself and so lovely to eat raw. In this technicolour salad the red cabbage and peppery rocket counteract the sweetness of the beetroot, which in any case is less pronounced when raw.

2 small fresh beetroot, peeled and coarsely grated
100 g / 4 oz red cabbage, shredded
2 red Roasted Peppers (page 178), diced
½ red onion, very thinly sliced into rings
1 fresh red chilli, seeded and finely chopped
1 clove Roasted Garlic (page 183), finely chopped
4 tbsp snipped fresh chives
Balsamic Vinaigrette (page 187)
salt and freshly ground black pepper
4–5 handfuls trimmed rocket or watercress
Grilled Polenta (page 185), cut into squares or diamonds
4–6 streaky bacon rashers, grilled until crisp

In a large bowl, combine the beetroot, cabbage, red peppers, onion, chilli, garlic and chives. Toss with the vinaigrette and check the seasoning.

Arrange the rocket on individual plates. Place 1–2 pieces of grilled polenta in the middle and pile the beetroot mixture on top. Sprinkle with crumbled bacon.

CARPACCIO OF ROOTS WITH WALNUTS

SERVES 2–3

Use a very sharp knife or mandoline to slice the vegetables into paper-thin slices.

½ mooli (Dutch white radish)
2 carrots
1 small parsnip
1 small kohlrabi
3 large radishes
4 spring onions, green parts included, chopped
40 g/1½ oz walnuts, coarsely chopped
Walnut Citrus Dressing (page 195)
1 Little Gem lettuce
2–3 handfuls lamb's lettuce
salt and freshly ground black pepper
mustard and cress, to garnish

Peel all the vegetables, then slice them horizontally into paper-thin circles. Transfer to a shallow dish with the spring onions and walnuts.

Add the dressing and toss well. Leave to stand for at least 30 minutes at room temperature.

Divide the salad greens between individual plates and pile the vegetables on top. Season to taste and garnish with mustard and cress.

SALAD OF MIXED ROOT VEGETABLES WITH ROASTED PEPPER AND YOGURT SAUCE, PEANUTS AND GREEN BEANS

SERVES 2

Be adventurous in your choice of root vegetables – they all have subtly different flavours. Try any or all of the following: celeriac, parsnips, kohlrabi, potatoes, yams or eddoes. The vegetables and the sauce should be served just warm or at room temperature. Add a serving of zesty Tomato and Cucumber Salsa (page 169) if you like – it contrasts well with the soft earthiness of the root vegetables.

700 g/1½ lb mixed root vegetables
lemon juice
1 small cos lettuce
100 g/4 oz cooked green beans, roughly chopped
2 red cocktail onions, thinly sliced
olive oil
salt and freshly ground black pepper
Roasted Pepper and Yogurt Sauce (page 201)
25 g/1 oz toasted peanuts, coarsely chopped
2 tbsp chopped fresh flat-leafed parsley

Peel the vegetables and cut into even-sized 5 mm/¼ inch slices. As you work, put them in a bowl of water with lemon juice added to prevent discolouration.

Put the vegetables in a steamer basket with the denser ones at the bottom. Steam over boiling water for 7–8 minutes, until only just tender. Spread them out carefully on a plate, sprinkle with lemon juice and allow to cool a little.

Tear the lettuce into bite-sized pieces and divide between individual plates. Arrange the root vegetables in the middle and scatter the beans and onions round the edge.

Sprinkle with more lemon juice, drizzle with olive oil and season to taste. Spoon some of the sauce over the roots and sprinkle with the peanuts and parsley.

WHITE WINTER SALAD WITH CORIANDER AND BRAZIL NUTS

SERVES 2–3

Fibre-rich crunchy root vegetables are great for winter salads. You'll need about 350 g/12 oz prepared vegetables in total. Root vegetables are loaded with carbohydrate to boost your energy, and contain useful vitamins and minerals such as potassium, iron, vitamin C and folate. The salad also contains a fair amount of garlic, which is known to protect against infection. This would be good served with fresh or Oven-Dried Tomatoes (page 157) and some leftover cooked ham or beef. You could also add one or two small salads, such as Mushroom and Coriander Salad (page 162) or Green Bean, Lemon and Sesame Salad (page 163).

½ celeriac
1 small kohlrabi
1 small parsnip
1 small mooli (Dutch white radish)
lemon juice
150 ml/¼ pint Greek yogurt
2 garlic cloves, finely chopped
3 tbsp chopped fresh coriander
¼ tsp coarse sea salt
freshly ground black pepper
25 g/1 oz toasted Brazil nuts, roughly chopped

Thinly slice the celeriac and kohlrabi. Stack a few slices at a time and cut into small segments. Cut the parsnip and the mooli into thin diagonal slices. As you work, immediately plunge each vegetable into a bowl of water to which you have added lemon juice to prevent browning.

Combine the yogurt, garlic, coriander, salt and pepper with 1 teaspoon of lemon juice, or to taste.

Drain the vegetables and quickly pat dry with paper towel. Put in a serving bowl and toss with the yogurt mixture. Scatter over the Brazil nuts and serve immediately.

SPICY ROASTED POTATO SALAD

SERVES 2

The potatoes are deliciously spicy and crisp – rather like large roasted chips. Serve them warm or at room temperature.

2 large floury potatoes, unpeeled
4 tbsp olive oil
½ tsp paprika
generous pinch of cayenne
½ tsp dried oregano
salt and freshly ground black pepper
1 small cos lettuce
Tomato and Avocado Salsa (page 170)
Cucumber and Yogurt (page 167)

Boil the potatoes in their skins for 10 minutes. Drain and allow to cool slightly. Peel off the skins and cut each potato lengthways into 8 equal-sized segments.

Heat the oil in a roasting tin until very hot. Add the potatoes, spreading them out in a single layer. Sprinkle with paprika, cayenne, oregano, and salt and pepper to taste, turning so they are well coated.

Roast in a preheated oven at 220°C/425°F/gas 7 for 45 minutes, turning occasionally, until golden and crisp. Remove from the tin and drain on paper towel. Allow to cool slightly.

Arrange the lettuce on individual plates with the potatoes on top. Add a serving of tomato and avocado salsa and spoon the cucumber and yogurt over the potatoes.

CAULIFLOWER, GREEN BEAN AND ALMOND SALAD WITH FENNEL AND MINT

SERVES 2–3

Serve the cauliflower and beans slightly warm or at room temperature. This is good served as part of a selection of vegetable salads such as Kohlrabi Salad with Lemon and Lovage (page 155), Mushroom and Coriander Salad (page 162), or Potato Salad with Yogurt and Mint (page 165).

275 g/10 oz cauliflower florets
100 g/4 oz green beans, trimmed and cut into 2.5 cm/1 inch pieces
1/4 tsp toasted fennel seeds, crushed
finely grated zest and juice of ½ lemon
1 clove Roasted Garlic (page 183), finely chopped
3 tbsp extra virgin olive oil
1/4 tsp dried chilli flakes
1 tbsp chopped fresh mint
1 tbsp chopped fresh chives
25 g/1 oz almonds with skins, toasted and sliced lengthways
salt and freshly ground black pepper

Trim the cauliflower florets where the heads meet the stalk. Put in a steamer basket with the beans and steam over boiling water for 3 minutes until only just tender.

Put the cauliflower and beans in a serving bowl while still warm, and toss with the remaining ingredients.

MUSHROOM AND BROAD BEAN SALAD WITH MINT

SERVES 2–3

Broad beans contain all the anti-oxidant vitamins (vitamins A, E and C) as well as useful minerals. Frozen ones are just as nutritious, but there is nothing to beat freshly picked young beans for flavour. If you are using fresh beans, you will need about 900 g/2 lb unshelled. Don't use large ones as they can be tough and mealy.

4 tbsp olive oil
225 g/8 oz assorted mushrooms, such as chestnut, oyster, shiitake,
cut into 1 cm/½ inch pieces
2 garlic cloves, finely chopped
1 shallot, finely chopped
2 tbsp sherry vinegar
4 tbsp chopped fresh mint
salt and freshly ground black pepper
225 g/8 oz frozen or shelled fresh broad beans
1 handful each lamb's lettuce and rocket
1 Little Gem lettuce
Garlic Croutons (page 184)

Heat 3 tablespoons of the oil in a frying pan until very hot. Add the mushrooms and stir-fry over a high heat for 3–4 minutes. Remove from the pan with a slotted spoon and transfer to a bowl.

Heat the remaining oil in the same pan and stir-fry the garlic and shallot over a high heat for 50–60 seconds. Do not allow the garlic to burn. Stir in the vinegar, scraping up any residue from the bottom of the pan. Add the mint and season to taste. Pour the mixture over the mushrooms.

Steam the beans over boiling water for 2–3 minutes. Drain under cold running water and pat dry. Slip off the outer skins if they are tough. Add the beans to the mushrooms.

Put the salad greens in a bowl and toss with the mushrooms and beans. Add a few croutons and check the seasoning. Add a little more olive oil if necessary.

WARM SALAD OF GRILLED MUSHROOMS, RED PEPPER AND ROCKET

SERVES 2

For a gastronomic high, make this in the autumn with a selection of freshly gathered wild mushrooms, such as ceps, bolitus and parasols. But make sure you can identify them accurately. Otherwise use a good selection of cultivated mushrooms. Allow 1–2 hours for marinating.

350 g/12 oz mixed wild or cultivated mushrooms
1 head radicchio, torn into bite-sized pieces
2 handfuls trimmed rocket
½ red Roasted Pepper (page 178), cut into thin strips
2 oil-cured bottled artichokes, quartered
salt and freshly ground black pepper
warm Polenta Croutons (page 185)

MARINADE
2 garlic cloves, finely chopped
1 tbsp chopped fresh thyme
2 tbsp lemon juice
2 tbsp soy sauce
2 tsp balsamic vinegar
6 tbsp olive oil
freshly ground black pepper

Cut the mushrooms into even-sized pieces. Put in a single layer in a shallow dish into which they will just fit. Whisk the marinade ingredients and pour over the mushrooms. Marinate at room temperature for 1–2 hours.

Drain the mushrooms, reserving the marinade. Put the

marinade in a small saucepan. Simmer for 2 minutes over a medium heat. Keep warm.

Thread the mushrooms onto skewers. Place on a rack under a preheated very hot grill or over hot coals. Grill for 3–5 minutes on each side, turning once. Remove from the skewers and keep warm.

Arrange the radicchio and rocket in a shallow serving dish or on individual plates. Add the red pepper, artichokes and mushrooms, then season. Spoon over a little of the warmed marinade and scatter with polenta croutons. Serve at once.

BROAD BEAN, SPINACH AND CHERRY TOMATO SALAD

SERVES 2

Broad beans are so full of vitamins and minerals that it's worth making this with frozen broad beans when fresh ones are out of season. Savory seems to go particularly well with broad beans, perhaps because it is traditionally grown as a companion plant to discourage blackfly. You could use mint instead but the flavour will be different.

225 g/8 oz shelled young broad beans (about 900 g/2 lb unshelled)
2 tsp chopped fresh summer savory
finely grated zest of ½ lemon
2 tbsp olive oil
coarse sea salt and freshly ground black pepper
4 handfuls young spinach, trimmed and torn into bite-sized pieces
100 g/4 oz cherry tomatoes
2 red cocktail onions, thinly sliced
12 pitted black olives
2 hard-boiled eggs, sliced
snipped fresh chives, to garnish

Steam the broad beans over boiling water for 2–3 minutes until only just cooked. Drain under cold running water and pat dry. Slip off their outer skins if they are tough. Toss with the savory, lemon zest, 1 tablespoon of the oil, and salt and pepper.

Toss the spinach and tomatoes with the remaining oil. Arrange on individual plates with the beans on top. Add the onions, olives and hard-boiled egg slices. Sprinkle the eggs with chives.

AVOCADO, RED ONION AND ROASTED PEPPER SALAD

SERVES 2

The fat in the avocado adds substance to this light and zesty salad. The fat is mono-unsaturated – the kind which doesn't clog your arteries. Avocados are also rich in vitamin E.

4 handfuls mixed salad greens, such as watercress, red oak
lettuce, batavia
1 red Roasted Pepper (page 178), diced
6 radishes, sliced
½ red onion, thinly sliced
Lime and Coriander Dressing (page 198)
1 large avocado, halved and thinly sliced crossways
1 small fresh green chilli, seeded and finely chopped
10 pitted black olives
coriander leaves, to garnish

Combine the salad greens, pepper, radishes and onion in a bowl and toss with a little of the dressing. Arrange on individual plates and top with the avocado slices. Drizzle with a little more dressing. Scatter over the chilli and olives, and garnish with coriander.

AUBERGINE, RED PEPPER AND WATER CHESTNUT SALAD

SERVES 2–3

A colourful salad with an oriental flavour. The crunchy water chestnuts are delicious with the soft, rich aubergines.

2 small aubergines
olive oil
½ red pepper, seeded and finely diced
Japanese Horseradish Vinaigrette (page 197)
2 tbsp sesame oil
225 g/8 oz can water chestnuts, drained and halved
½ tbsp shoyu
salt and freshly ground black pepper
75 g/3 oz mangetout, trimmed
½ head Chinese leaves, shredded
1 tsp toasted sesame seeds
4 spring onions, sliced diagonally into 2 cm/¾ inch lengths
6 radishes, sliced

Rub the aubergines with oil and roast in a preheated oven at 230°C/450°F/gas 8 for 20 minutes until soft. Allow to cool, then remove the skin and slice lengthways into eighths, discarding any clumps of seeds. Slice diagonally into 5 cm/2 inch strips. Put in a bowl with the pepper and toss with 3 tablespoons of the dressing.

Heat the sesame oil in a small pan and stir-fry the water chestnuts over a high heat for 3 minutes. Add the shoyu and seasoning and fry for another minute. Remove from the pan with a slotted spoon and add to the aubergines.

Plunge the mangetout into boiling water for 1 minute. Drain

under cold running water, pat dry and slice diagonally into three.

Make a bed of Chinese leaves on a serving dish or individual plates. Pile the aubergine mixture in the middle and sprinkle with the sesame seeds. Scatter the spring onions, radishes and mangetout round the edge, and spoon over a little more dressing.

CALIFORNIAN SALAD PLATTER

SERVES 2

Great for slimmers just as it is, or add hot, spicy Guacamole (page 174) and serve with tortilla chips for extra substance.

1 large avocado
1 kiwi fruit
1 papaya
4 handfuls mixed leaves, such as rocket, mizuna, radicchio
1 tbsp chopped fresh mixed herbs
25 g / 1 oz toasted hazelnuts, roughly chopped
Hazelnut and Lime Dressing (page 197)
herbs sprigs, to garnish

Thinly slice the avocado, kiwi fruit and papaya. Put in a salad bowl with the leaves, herbs and half the hazelnuts. Toss with the dressing, scatter with the remaining nuts and garnish with herb sprigs.

SPINACH GARDEN SALAD

SERVES 2

Raw spinach plays an important part in healthy salads. The deep emerald green leaves are packed with carotene (vitamin A), folate and vitamin C, together with essential minerals such as potassium, calcium, iron and zinc.

4 handfuls young spinach, trimmed and torn into bite-sized pieces
2 chestnut mushrooms, thinly sliced
4 small celery stalks (from the centre of the bunch), leaves included, sliced
2 spring onions, sliced lengthways into 4
Garlic Croutons (page 184)
Balsamic Vinaigrette (page 187)
2 hard-boiled eggs, sliced
4 grilled streaky bacon rashers, crumbled

Combine the spinach, mushrooms, celery, spring onions and croutons in a large bowl. Add enough dressing to just coat the leaves and toss well. Top with the eggs and crumbled bacon pieces and drizzle with a little more dressing.

GADO-GADO

SERVES 3–4

This is a classic Indonesian salad of cooked and raw vegetables with a spicy peanut dressing. To blanch the vegetables, plunge them together into a large saucepan of briskly boiling salted water. Immediately remove from the heat and drain under cold running water to stop further cooking. Pat dry with paper towel. The vegetables should be very crisp and brightly coloured. The salad would be good served with rice, or rice noodles tossed in a little sesame oil.

4 waxy new potatoes, cooked and sliced
100 g/4 oz green beans, cut into 2.5 cm/1 inch lengths and blanched
2 carrots, cut lengthways into eighths, then into 4 cm/1½ inch
pieces, blanched
100 g/4 oz broccoli florets, stalks included and thinly sliced, blanched
225 g/8 oz finely shredded cabbage, blanched
¼ cucumber, unpeeled, cut into strips
175 g/6 oz bean sprouts
coarse sea salt
Caramelised Onion Rings (page 175), optional
2 hard-boiled eggs, quartered
Indonesian Peanut Dressing (page 202)
fresh coriander leaves, to garnish

Arrange the potatoes in a shallow serving dish or on individual plates. Add the other vegetables and season to taste with salt. Scatter over a few onion rings and top with the eggs. Spoon over some of the dressing and serve the rest in a jug. Garnish with coriander leaves.

2

Fish and Seafood Salads

Adding fish or seafood to a salad not only creates new depths of flavour and texture, but provides extra essential nutrients. All fish and seafood are a good source of protein and valuable minerals – calcium, iron and zinc. Oily fish, such as trout, mackerel and tuna, contain fat-soluble vitamins A and D, and a particular type of essential fatty acid thought to protect against heart disease. Shellfish provide B vitamins, which are needed for the release of energy from food within the body.

However, fish and seafood are low in fibre, carbohydrate and vitamin C. To make up the deficiency, many of these salads include starchy vegetables, grains and nuts, together with salad leaves or fruit. You may wish to supplement them further with additional small salads, salsas and dips.

ORIENTAL PRAWN SALAD

SERVES 2-3

A light lunchtime salad, full of fresh flavours and crunchy texture. You could add some rice noodles tossed in a little sesame oil for extra substance.

½ small cucumber
¼ head Chinese leaves, thinly sliced
½ packet trimmed watercress
50 g/2 oz button mushrooms, thinly sliced
50 g/2 oz bean sprouts
5 radishes, thinly sliced
Oriental Vinaigrette (page 189)
175 g/6 oz cooked shelled tiger prawns
chopped spring onion tops, to garnish
½ tsp toasted sesame seeds

Peel away alternate strips of skin from the cucumber, then slice thinly.

Put the cucumber, Chinese leaves, watercress, mushrooms, bean sprouts and radishes in a shallow serving dish or on individual plates, and toss with some of the dressing.

Arrange the prawns on top and garnish with spring onion tops. Sprinkle with the sesame seeds and drizzle with a little more dressing.

PRAWN AND AVOCADO SALAD WITH GARLIC MAYONNAISE

SERVES 2–3

You could use Coriander and Chilli Cream (page 202), or Avocado and Smoked Tofu Dip (page 173) as alternatives to garlic mayonnaise.

2 handfuls frisee
2 plum tomatoes, halved and cut into segments
4 mushrooms, thinly sliced
75 g/3 oz cooked green beans, cut into 2 cm/¾ inch pieces
½ red pepper, cut into matchstick strips
1 head chicory, sliced lengthways
1 tbsp chopped fresh mixed herbs
extra virgin olive oil
salt and freshly ground black pepper
1 avocado
lemon juice
3 garlic cloves, crushed
1 tbsp mayonnaise
1 tbsp Greek yogurt
cayenne
100 g/4 oz large shelled cooked prawns
1 or 2 large unshelled cooked prawns, to decorate

Put the frisee, tomatoes, mushrooms, beans, pepper and chicory in a large bowl. Add the herbs and toss with just enough olive oil to coat. Season to taste.

Half the avocado and slice lengthways. Sprinkle with a little lemon juice.

Mix the garlic, mayonnaise, yogurt and cayenne.

Arrange the salad on a serving dish or individual plates. Top with slices of avocado and the prawns. Use the unshelled prawns for decoration. Spoon the garlic mayonnaise over the prawns and serve at once.

GRILLED PRAWN SALAD WITH PALM HEARTS

SERVES 2

It's worth keeping a can of palm hearts in your storecupboard as they make an unusual and delicious addition to a salad. However, unless you're feeding a crowd it's difficult to use up the whole can at once. Unused portions can be covered with water and kept in the fridge for a few days, added to salads or served on their own with mayonnaise.

1½ tbsp shoyu
1 tbsp dry sherry
2 garlic cloves, finely chopped
¼–½ tsp dried chilli flakes
juice of 1 lime
pinch of salt
175 g/6 oz uncooked tiger prawns with shells, heads removed
75 g/3 oz mangetout, trimmed
100 g/4 oz drained canned palm hearts
toasted sesame oil
½ yellow pepper, seeded and cut into very thin strips
½ avocado, thinly sliced
½ head Chinese leaves, torn into bite-sized pieces
Hazelnut and Lime Dressing (page 197)
coriander leaves, to garnish
fresh red chilli, to garnish

Combine the shoyu, sherry, garlic, chilli, lime juice and salt in a small bowl. Add the prawns and marinate for at least 1 hour.

Plunge the mangetout into boiling water, then drain immediately under cold running water and pat dry. Cut into thin diagonal slices. Cut the palm hearts into thin diagonal slices.

Thread the prawns on skewers, brush with sesame oil and grill for 3 minutes each side.

Put the palm hearts, mangetout, pepper, avocado and Chinese leaves in a bowl and toss with just enough dressing to coat.

Arrange the salad on individual plates. Remove the prawns from their skewers and scatter on top. Drizzle over a few drops of sesame oil and garnish with fresh coriander and chilli.

PRAWN, RED CABBAGE, RADISH AND RICE SALAD

SERVES 2–3

A beautiful salad of pinks and deep reds, with crisp crunchy
vegetables and meaty prawns.

2 garlic cloves, finely chopped
3 tbsp rice vinegar
3 tbsp unrefined sunflower oil, or olive oil
1 tbsp shoyu or tamari
200 g/7 oz large cooked shelled prawns
250 g/9 oz cooked white or brown long-grain rice (about 90 g/3½ oz
uncooked)
200 g/7 oz finely shredded red cabbage
175 g/6 oz trimmed radishes, finely sliced
75 g/3 oz bean sprouts
2 spring onions, green parts included, shredded
toasted sesame seeds

Whisk the garlic, rice vinegar, sunflower oil and shoyu in a
small bowl. Put the prawns in another bowl and toss with 2
tablespoons of the dressing. Leave to marinate for at least 30
minutes.

Put the rice in a bowl with the cabbage, radishes and bean
sprouts. Toss with 3 tablespoons of the dressing.

Divide the rice mixture between individual plates and top
with the drained prawns. Garnish with the spring onions and
sprinkle with sesame seeds.

SCALLOP AND ARTICHOKE SALAD WITH HAZELNUTS

SERVES 2

The warm, fragrant raspberry vinegar dressing makes this a particularly delicious salad. Scallops contain plenty of protein, hardly any fat, and are rich in iron, zinc and selenium.

2–3 handfuls red oak lettuce, torn into bite-sized pieces
1 handful each of lamb's lettuce and trimmed watercress
6 oil-cured bottled baby artichokes, quartered
2 red cocktail onions, thinly sliced
2 tbsp safflower or sunflower oil
8 scallops, sliced horizontally in half
50 g/2 oz toasted hazelnuts, roughly chopped
4 tbsp hazelnut oil
1 tbsp raspberry vinegar
salt and freshly ground black pepper

Divide the red oak lettuce, lamb's lettuce and watercress between individual plates. Top with the artichokes and sprinkle with the onions.

Heat the safflower oil in a pan. Add the scallops and fry over a medium-high heat for about 1 minute each side. Do not overcook. Arrange the scallops on the plates and sprinkle with the hazelnuts.

Warm the hazelnut oil and vinegar in the same pan and spoon over the scallops. Season to taste and serve at once.

ORIENTAL SQUID SALAD WITH NOODLES

SERVES 2

A salad of bright colours and zesty flavours. If you don't have squid, use prawns or cooked mixed seafood instead. The palm hearts could be substituted with blanched mangetout. Use plenty of Chinese leaf stalk for a lovely peppery texture.

225 g/8 oz cleaned squid
75 g/3 oz thin Chinese egg noodles, cooked and drained
½ head Chinese leaves, shredded
1 red pepper, finely diced
50 g/2 oz drained canned palm hearts, thinly sliced
diagonally
1–2 red Roasted Chillies (page 182), finely diced
4 spring onions, green parts included,
finely chopped
2 tbsp chopped fresh coriander
2 tbsp chopped fresh mint
5 cm/2 inch piece fresh ginger root
6 tbsp olive oil
2 tbsp toasted sesame oil
2 garlic cloves, crushed
2 tsp shoyu
salt and freshly ground black pepper

Cut the squid into 1 cm/½ inch rings but leave the tentacles whole. Plunge the rings and the tentacles into boiling water and simmer briefly for 2–3 minutes until tender. Be careful not to overcook. Drain immediately under cold running water and pat dry with paper towel.

Put the squid, noodles, Chinese leaves, red pepper, palm

hearts, chilli, spring onions, coriander and mint in a serving bowl.

Put the ginger in a garlic press and squeeze the juice into a small bowl. Whisk in the oils, garlic, shoyu and seasoning. Pour over the salad and toss well.

MIXED SEAFOOD SALAD WITH ORIENTAL NOODLES

SERVES 2

Seafood cocktail – mussels, prawns, squid, crab sticks – can be bought at most large supermarkets. It can be fairly tasteless – zapping it up with a marinade makes all the difference.

350 g/12 oz cooked seafood cocktail
75 g/3 oz flat cellophane noodles or rice noodles
1½ tsp toasted sesame oil
1–2 handfuls pungent leaves, such as rocket, watercress or Japanese mustard greens
50 g/2 oz cucumber, cut into matchstick strips
4 radishes, thinly sliced and cut into strips
Oriental Vinaigrette (page 189)
1 tbsp roasted peanuts, roughly chopped

MARINADE
juice of 1 lime
1 tbsp chopped fresh coriander
1 tbsp chopped fresh mint
¼ tsp dried chilli flakes
1 garlic clove
¼ tsp sugar
2 tbsp shoyu
1 tbsp olive oil
½ tsp toasted sesame oil

Combine the marinade ingredients in a bowl. Add the seafood and marinate in the refrigerator for at least 1 hour.

Cook the noodles according to the packet instructions. Drain under cold running water. Cut into 15 cm/6 inch lengths and pat dry with paper towel. Put in a bowl and toss with the sesame oil.

Arrange the noodles on individual plates, with the leaves around the edge. Drain the seafood and place on top of the noodles. Scatter over the cucumber and radishes.

Spoon over some of the dressing and sprinkle with the peanuts. Serve at once.

TUNA AND RICE SALAD WITH ROASTED PEPPER AND CHILLI

SERVES 2–3

I have used canned tuna for convenience, but chargrilled fresh tuna would turn this into something really special. If you don't have roasted peppers and chillies to hand, use fresh ones instead, but the salad won't have that smoky flavour.

350 g/12 oz cooked white long-grain rice
(about 150 g/5 oz uncooked)
1 yellow Roasted Pepper (page 178), diced
1 Roasted Chilli (page 182), diced
2 tomatoes, peeled, seeded and diced
3 spring onions, finely chopped
2 tbsp chopped fresh coriander
Cumin and Lime Vinaigrette (page 190)
2–3 handfuls mixed green salad leaves
200 g/7 oz can tuna fish, drained and flaked
2 hard-boiled eggs, quartered
pitted black olives, to garnish

Put the rice in a bowl with the pepper, chilli, tomatoes, spring onions and coriander. Pour the dressing over and toss gently.

Pile the mixture on a bed of salad leaves, and arrange the tuna, eggs and olives on top.

TUNA, CUCUMBER AND SEA VEGETABLE SALAD

SERVES 2-3

High in fibre, low in fat, sea vegetables are an unbelievably rich source of essential minerals needed by the body. Sea vegetables may taste a bit strange at first, but arame and hiziki are good ones for beginners to try. They are both mild flavoured, and very rich in calcium and iron. Cooking the sea vegetables can be done in advance.

15 g/½ oz dried arame or hiziki
1 tbsp sunflower oil
1 tbsp shoyu
⅓ cucumber
2 × 175 g/6 oz cans tuna, drained and flaked
1 tbsp lemon juice
4 spring onions, green parts included, sliced diagonally
Oriental Vinaigrette (page 189)
3 radishes, sliced
1 tsp toasted sesame seeds

Rinse the arame and soak in 425 ml/¾ pint of cold water for 20 minutes. Drain, reserving the soaking water.

Heat the oil and stir-fry the arame for 5 minutes. Add the shoyu and 300 ml/½ pint of the soaking water. Simmer briskly for about 25 minutes until the liquid has almost evaporated. Spread out on a plate and leave to cool.

Slice the cucumber, then stack a few slices at a time and cut into quarters.

Put the tuna in a serving bowl and sprinkle with lemon juice. Carefully toss with the cucumber, arame and spring onions. Spoon over the vinaigrette, top with the radishes and sprinkle with the sesame seeds.

SALAD OF WARM TUNA, MIXED BEANS AND ARTICHOKES WITH ROSEMARY AND LIME

SERVES 2

If you like rosemary, as I do, this is the salad for you. The beans really take on the flavour. Prepare the beans ahead of time and let them sit in the dressing for as long as possible.

6 tbsp olive oil
3 tbsp lime juice
¼–½ tsp dried chilli flakes
freshly ground black pepper
2 thin fresh tuna steaks, weighing 100–150 g/4–5 oz each
75 g/3 oz mixed dried beans, such as flageolet and kidney,
soaked overnight
salt
1 tbsp walnut oil
1 shallot, finely chopped
1 garlic clove, very finely chopped
1½ tsp finely chopped fresh rosemary
1 tbsp chopped fresh flat-leafed parsley
3 handfuls escarole or frisee, torn into bite-sized pieces
2 handfuls trimmed rocket
2 oil-cured bottled artichokes, quartered
2 plum tomatoes, cut lengthways into segments
8 pitted black olives
lime wedges, to garnish

Put 3 tablespoons of the olive oil in a bowl with 2 tablespoons of the lime juice, the chilli and pepper. Add the tuna steaks and marinate for at least 1 hour, turning occasionally.

Meanwhile, drain the beans and put in a saucepan with

enough water to cover. Bring to the boil, then boil rapidly for 20 minutes. Continue to cook until tender, adding salt during the last 10 minutes of cooking time.

Drain the beans. While still warm toss with 2 tablespoons of the olive oil, the walnut oil, shallot, garlic, rosemary, parsley, remaining lime juice, and salt and pepper to taste. Leave to stand for at least 30 minutes.

Heat the remaining oil in a pan until very hot. Sear the tuna for 1–2 minutes each side over a very high heat. Remove from the pan and allow to cool a little.

Toss the escarole and rocket with the beans. Arrange in a serving dish or on individual plates. Add the artichokes, tomatoes and olives, adding more oil and seasoning if necessary. Flake the tuna and add to the salad. Garnish with lime wedges and serve at once.

SALADE NICOISE

SERVES 3–4

A classic Mediterranean salad with numerous variations depending on the season and availability of ingredients. Blanched baby broad beans, sliced green or red peppers, capers and anchovies would be good additions or alternatives, but the potatoes, eggs and tuna are essential.

6 handfuls crisp lettuce, such as batavia, iceberg or cos, torn into
bite-sized pieces
6–8 cooked waxy potatoes, sliced
100 g/4 oz blanched green beans, chopped
2 tsp each chopped fresh basil, chives and flat-leafed parsley
1 garlic clove, crushed
Basic Vinaigrette (page 187)
4 tomatoes, quartered
3 oil-cured bottled artichokes, quartered
2–3 hard-boiled eggs, quartered
2 × 175 g/6 oz cans tuna, drained and flaked
pitted black olives, to garnish
basil leaves, to garnish

Line a shallow serving dish with the lettuce. Add the potatoes and beans.

Whisk the herbs and the garlic with the dressing, and drizzle a little over the salad.

Add the tomatoes, artichokes, eggs and tuna. Garnish with olives and basil, and pour over some more dressing. Serve at room temperature.

CEVICHE

SERVES 2–3

Don't be put off by raw fish. The lime juice makes it taste and look cooked, and maximum nutrients are retained. However, to avoid tummy upsets, the fish must be extremely fresh. Use any firm-fleshed fish, such as halibut, shark or monkfish.

225 g/8 oz firm white fish, skinned and cut into small chunks
2 tbsp lime juice
100 g/4 oz large shelled cooked prawns
3 plum tomatoes, peeled, seeded and diced
½ green pepper, diced
½ small red onion, thinly sliced
1 small green chilli, seeded and diced
2 tbsp chopped fresh coriander or flat-leafed parsley
¼ tsp powdered or dried oregano
1 tbsp wine vinegar
3 tbsp extra virgin olive oil
salt and freshly ground black pepper
1 small cos lettuce, torn into bite-sized pieces
1 avocado, halved and sliced crossways
dash of Tabasco sauce
pitted black olives, to garnish

Put the fish and lime juice in a non-reactive bowl and marinate for 3–4 hours, turning occasionally.

Add the prawns, tomatoes, pepper, onion and chilli to the bowl, together with the parsley, oregano, vinegar, oil and seasoning.

Arrange the lettuce in a shallow serving dish or on individual plates. Add the fish mixture and top with the avocado. Add a sprinkling of Tabasco sauce, and garnish with olives.

MARINATED SARDINE SALAD WITH FENNEL AND TOMATO

SERVES 2

A salad of contrasting flavours and textures. The aniseedy fennel offsets the richness of the sardines, while the croutons add crunch and soak up the zesty juices.

8 fresh sardines, gutted
4 handfuls trimmed rocket or watercress
1 fennel bulb, quartered lengthways, cored and sliced into thin strips
4 tomatoes, cut into segments
Garlic Croutons (page 184) or Polenta Croutons (page 185)
6 strips oil-cured sun-dried tomato, chopped
torn basil leaves
pitted black olives, to garnish

MARINADE
6 tbsp extra virgin olive oil
juice of 1 lemon
1 tsp fennel seeds, toasted and crushed
2 bay leaves
¼ tsp dried chilli flakes
1 tsp sugar
1 tsp black peppercorns, crushed
¼ tsp coarse sea salt
1 small red onion, thinly sliced

Thread the sardines onto skewers and place under a very hot grill for 2–3 minutes each side. Carefully slide the sardines off the skewers and place in a shallow dish. Allow to cool a little.

Combine the marinade ingredients and pour over the fish.

Cover and marinate for at least 4 hours, or for up to 3 days in the fridge.

When ready to serve, arrange the rocket in a shallow dish or on individual plates. Add the fennel and tomatoes, and top with the sardines and a few croutons. Spoon over the onion from the marinade and some of the liquid. Sprinkle with the sun-dried tomato and basil, and garnish with olives.

GRILLED SARDINE, BEAN AND POTATO SALAD

SERVES 2

Cheap and quickly prepared, sardines make a particularly healthy addition to a salad. They are bursting with minerals such as potassium, calcium, iron, zinc and selenium, and are a rich source of vitamins D, E, niacin (vitamin B3) and B12.

6–8 small fresh sardines, gutted
juice of 1 lemon
¼ tsp dried chilli flakes
salt and freshly ground black pepper
2 handfuls bitter and pungent salad leaves, such as frisee or escarole,
torn into bite-sized pieces
100 g/4 oz cooked green beans, chopped
4 cooked new potatoes, sliced
6 red cocktail onions, halved
10 cherry tomatoes
2 hard-boiled eggs, roughly chopped
1 tbsp snipped fresh chives
Basic Vinaigrette (page 187)
lemon wedges, to garnish

Thread the sardines on skewers and place under a very hot grill for 2–3 minutes each side. Remove from the skewers and put in a bowl. Sprinkle with the lemon juice, chilli flakes, and salt and pepper.

Arrange the salad leaves in a shallow serving dish or on individual plates. Add the beans, potatoes, onions, tomatoes and eggs. Sprinkle with the chives and drizzle with enough vinaigrette to coat. Add the sardines and garnish with lemon wedges.

MEDITERRANEAN FISH SALAD

SERVES 2

Pumpkin seed oil adds a wonderfully rich flavour to the salad, but you could use good quality extra virgin olive oil instead.

150 g/5 oz each monkfish and squid
100 g/4 oz uncooked prawns with shells, peeled and deveined
juice of 1–2 lemons
8 tbsp extra virgin olive oil
2 garlic cloves, crushed
½ tsp dried chilli flakes
salt and freshly ground black pepper
2 handfuls trimmed rocket
1 Oven-Dried Aubergine (page 177), cut into 2.5 cm/1 inch pieces
2 Roasted Courgettes (page 180), cut into chunks
1 red Roasted Pepper (page 178), cut into matchstick strips
2 spring onions, cut into 5 cm/2 inch pieces and shredded
1 fennel bulb, quartered, cored and thinly sliced
2 tbsp chopped fresh flat-leafed parsley
4–5 tbsp pumpkin seed oil
pitted black olives, to garnish

Cut the monkfish into chunks, and thinly slice the squid.

Combine 2 tablespoons of the lemon juice with the olive oil, garlic, chilli flakes and seasoning. Add all the fish and marinate for 1–2 hours in the fridge.

Thread the fish onto skewers. Place under a very hot grill for 5–7 minutes, brushing with the marinade, until just cooked.

Arrange the rocket, aubergine, courgettes, pepper, onions and fennel in a shallow serving dish or on individual plates. Sprinkle with the parsley and a squeeze of lemon juice. Drizzle with the pumpkin seed oil and top with the fish. Garnish with the olives and serve at once.

TROUT AND NEW POTATO SALAD

SERVES 2

You could add to this one of the small mixed vegetable salads such as Kohlrabi Salad with Lemon and Lovage (page 155), Marinated Carrot Ribbons (page 159) or Green Bean, Lemon and Sesame Salad (page 163).

200 g / 7 oz cooked flaked trout
8 cherry tomatoes
6–8 cooked new potatoes, sliced
2–3 handfuls trimmed watercress
75 g / 3 oz cucumber, thinly sliced
2 tender celery stalks, leaves included, sliced
extra virgin olive oil
Horseradish and Lemon Dressing (page 199)

Arrange all the ingredients on individual plates. Drizzle with a little olive oil and top the trout with a dollop of horseradish and lemon dressing.

WARM SMOKED TROUT AND HAZELNUT SALAD

SERVES 2

This is a quickly made salad of contrasting textures and flavours – crunchy sweet hazelnuts, tender trout and slightly bitter leaves, sharpened with a citrus dressing.

2 handfuls red oak lettuce, torn into bite-sized pieces
2 handfuls frisee
4 mushrooms, thinly sliced
Orange Vinaigrette (page 192)
1 tbsp grapeseed or sunflower oil
25 g / 1 oz shelled hazelnuts, roughly chopped
2 smoked trout fillets
squeeze of orange juice
freshly ground black pepper

Put the salad leaves and mushrooms in a bowl. Toss with just enough dressing to barely coat the leaves.

Heat the grapeseed oil in a pan. Add the hazelnuts and fry until beginning to brown. Add the trout fillets and warm through for about 2 minutes. Sprinkle with orange juice and a few grindings of black pepper.

Add to the salad with the juices from the pan. Serve at once.

SALAD OF GRILLED RED MULLET, GARLIC, FENNEL AND TOMATO

SERVES 2

Red mullet is rich in selenium, an important trace mineral.

2–4 red mullet
2 tsp toasted fennel seeds, crushed
lemon juice
2 tbsp olive oil
4 large garlic cloves, sliced
1 small cos lettuce, inner leaves only
1 fennel bulb, trimmed, cored and thinly sliced
1 large plum tomato, cut lengthways into segments
8 pitted black olives, sliced
2 tbsp grapeseed oil
2 tbsp walnut oil
2 tbsp sherry vinegar
salt and freshly ground black pepper
fennel fronds, to garnish

Score the fish lightly on each side with a sharp knife. Stuff the fennel seeds into the slits. Place the fish in a grill pan and sprinkle with lemon juice and half the olive oil.

Grill under a high heat for 4–5 minutes each side, then for 4–5 minutes under a moderate heat, basting with more oil and lemon juice. Remove from the heat and allow to cool slightly.

Heat the remaining olive oil in a small pan and gently fry the garlic for 2–3 minutes until just coloured. Do not allow it to burn or it will taste acrid and bitter.

Tear the lettuce into bite-sized pieces and arrange in a

serving dish or on individual plates. Add the fennel, tomato and olives.

Bone the fish, flake the flesh and add to the salad. Sprinkle with the garlic slices.

Gently warm the grapeseed oil with the walnut oil and vinegar. Season to taste and pour over the salad. Garnish with fennel fronds and serve at once.

CHARGRILLED SMOKED MACKEREL, RED PEPPER AND CELERIAC SALAD

SERVES 3–4

You can use smoked mackerel straight from the packet, but grilling reduces the fat content and gives a crisper texture.

4 large smoked mackerel fillets, halved lengthways
oil, for brushing
1 tsp fennel seeds, crushed
½ tsp dried chilli flakes
freshly ground black pepper
6 handfuls mixed salad leaves
Celeriac Remoulade (page 164)
1 red Roasted Pepper (page 178), cut into matchstick strips
50 g/2 oz cucumber, sliced and halved
2 tbsp lemon juice
parsley sprigs, to garnish

Brush the mackerel with oil and sprinkle with the fennel seeds, chilli flakes and pepper. Place under a very hot grill for about 8 minutes until beginning to blacken.

Make a bed of salad leaves in a shallow serving dish. Pile the celeriac in a line down the middle, with the red pepper and cucumber round the edge. Place the mackerel fillets diagonally on top. Sprinkle with the lemon juice and garnish with parsley sprigs.

SMOKED MACKEREL, BEETROOT AND PEANUT SALAD

SERVES 2

Add the beetroot at the last minute and position it exactly where you want it, otherwise the salad will be swimming in red juice. Unrefined roasted peanut oil has a wonderfully deep earthy flavour, which is delicious with the beetroot. If you don't have any, use a good quality extra virgin olive oil instead. Although high in fat, smoked mackerel is a good source of vitamin D and selenium, a valuable trace mineral. If you want to reduce the fat content, place the unskinned mackerel fillets on a rack under a very hot grill for about 8 minutes, turning once. Allow to cool, then add to the salad.

2 small raw beetroot, peeled and coarsely grated
4 tbsp salted peanuts, roughly chopped
3 tbsp roasted peanut (groundnut) oil
1 tbsp lemon juice
salt and freshly ground black pepper
2 handfuls young spinach, trimmed
2 handfuls red oak lettuce, torn into bite-sized pieces
4 small smoked mackerel fillets, skinned and flaked
3–4 small cooked potatoes, sliced
2–3 tbsp soured cream
snipped fresh chives, to garnish

Combine the beetroot, peanuts, oil, lemon juice and seasoning in a small bowl and set aside.

Arrange the spinach and lettuce on individual plates. Scatter the mackerel and potatoes around the edge and pile the beetroot mixture in the middle.

Spoon some soured cream over the mackerel and sprinkle the chives over the beetroot.

PICKLED HERRING, CELERY AND APPLE SALAD

SERVES 2–3

The herring mixture will keep for several days in the fridge. Although high in sodium, pickled herrings are a useful source of vitamins D, E and B complex.

1 crisp red-skinned apple, unpeeled
175 g/6 oz pickled herring fillets, cut into 2.5 cm/1 inch pieces
175 g/6 oz cooked potato, diced
4 tender celery stalks, sliced
6 cornichons (baby pickled cucumbers), sliced
6 tbsp plain yogurt
1 tbsp chopped fresh dill
2 tsp white wine vinegar
freshly ground black pepper
1 butterhead lettuce
handful of trimmed watercress
6 cucumber slices, halved

Cut the apple into eighths and remove the core. Slice crossways into segments. Put in a bowl with the herring, potato, celery and cornichons.

Combine the yogurt, dill, vinegar and pepper, and stir into the salad. Chill for at least 30 minutes.

When ready to serve, arrange the lettuce and watercress in a shallow serving dish or on individual plates. Pile the salad on top, and garnish with the cucumber slices. It is best served slightly chilled.

SALAD OF SMOKED EEL, PINK GRAPEFRUIT AND WALNUTS

SERVES 2

Eel is an acquired taste, but it is worth trying in small quantities as it is an exceptionally good source of retinol (vitamin A), and vitamins D and E. It also contains valuable minerals, such as iron, zinc and selenium. The oiliness of the eel is cut by the acidity of the grapefruit and the peppery leaves.

1 pink grapefruit
100 g / 4 oz smoked eel fillets, cut into thin 2 cm / ¾ inch strips
4 tender celery stalks, sliced
freshly ground black pepper
4 handfuls frisee
2 handfuls lamb's lettuce
extra virgin olive oil
25 g / 1 oz toasted walnut halves
Lemon Yogurt Dressing (page 198)
celery leaves, to garnish

Peel the grapefruit and remove the pith and seeds. Cut into slices and then into small segments.

Combine the grapefruit, eel and celery. Season to taste with pepper.

Toss the frisee and lamb's lettuce in just enough oil to barely coat the leaves. Arrange on individual plates and top with the eel mixture.

Sprinkle with the nuts and spoon over some of the dressing. Garnish with the celery leaves and serve at once.

SMOKED SALMON, PINK GRAPEFRUIT AND AVOCADO SALAD

SERVES 2

A very pretty salad, suitable for a light lunch. It's delicious served with fresh rye bread. For extra substance, you could add some cottage cheese or ricotta, generously seasoned with black pepper and chopped fresh herbs.

½ pink grapefruit
1 head radicchio
2–3 handfuls trimmed watercress
extra virgin olive oil
salt and freshly ground black pepper
100 g/4 oz smoked salmon, cut into strips
4 radishes, sliced
1 small avocado, diced
2 tsp chopped fresh dill or chives

Peel the grapefruit and remove the pith and seeds. Cut into thin slices, then into segments. Put in a small bowl and set aside.

Toss the radicchio and the watercress in a few drops of olive oil – enough to barely coat the leaves – and season with freshly ground black pepper and a pinch of salt. Arrange on individual plates.

Add the smoked salmon, grapefruit, radishes and avocado. Sprinkle with any grapefruit juice which has collected in the bowl. Drizzle over a little more oil and season with pepper. Sprinkle with dill or chives and serve at once.

SMOKED SALMON, PRAWN, ASPARAGUS AND WATERCRESS SALAD

SERVES 2

An elegant and light lunchtime salad with which you could serve some warm new potatoes, or the Potato Salad with Yogurt and Mint (page 165).

225 g/8 oz young asparagus
75 g/3 oz smoked salmon, cut into strips
100 g/4 oz shelled cooked prawns
4 mushrooms, thinly sliced
3 tender celery stalks (from the centre of the bunch), sliced lengthways into thin strips and then into 5 cm/2 inch pieces
2 handfuls trimmed watercress
4 handfuls crisp lettuce, torn into shreds
Japanese Horseradish Vinaigrette (page 194) or Basic Vinaigrette (page 187)

Plunge the asparagus into boiling water for 2–3 minutes. Drain under cold running water then pat dry. Cut off the tips and chop the stalks into 1 cm/½ inch pieces.

Arrange the asparagus stalks, salmon, prawns, mushrooms, celery, watercress and lettuce on individual plates. Drizzle with some of the dressing, arrange the asparagus tips on top and serve at once.

SMOKED SALMON, CUCUMBER AND RICOTTA SALAD

SERVES 2

Ricotta is a milky, mild, low-fat cheese – the ideal partner for salty smoked salmon. It should be very fresh, and look wet and white. If possible, buy it freshly made from an Italian delicatessen. Otherwise use the tubs sold in supermarkets.

¼ cucumber
salt
75 g/3 oz ricotta cheese
1 tbsp chopped fresh fennel or dill
freshly ground black pepper
100 g/4 oz smoked salmon, cut into 5 cm/2 inch
wide strips
2 handfuls trimmed watercress
2 handfuls frisee, torn into bite-sized pieces
6 cherry tomatoes, halved
squeeze of lemon juice
extra virgin olive oil
4 tbsp plain yogurt
1 tbsp whipping cream
finely grated zest of ½ lemon

Thinly slice the cucumber. Stack a few slices at a time and cut into matchstick strips. Put in a colander, sprinkle with salt and leave to drain for as long as possible. Rinse and pat dry with paper towel.

Beat the ricotta with half the fennel or dill and season to taste. Place a little of the mixture on one end of the smoked salmon pieces. Roll up carefully and chill.

Arrange the watercress, frisee and tomatoes on a serving dish or individual plates. Drizzle with lemon juice and a little oil.

Add the smoked salmon rolls. Arrange the cucumber strips over the salmon. Mix the yogurt, cream, lemon zest and remaining fennel or dill. Spoon the dressing over the salmon and cucumber.

3

Meat and Poultry Salads

Cold meat and poultry are traditional salad standbys. Here they are given new life with the addition of an exciting variety of flavourings – oriental dressings, robust vinegars and nut oils, fresh chillies, toasted nuts and spices, fresh herbs, fruit, relishes and pickles. The contrasting temperature of stir-fried or chargrilled meat, served warm on a bed of cool greens, further adds to the taste sensation.

Because of the saturated fat content, there is a tendency to exclude meat and poultry from health-promoting salads. However, the salads here use either lean cuts, or reduced quantities of the fattier types of meat, with minimum extra fat added during the cooking process. All meat and poultry are valuable sources of zinc, needed for healing processes, while red meat and game birds are rich in iron, often lacking in the Western diet.

With the addition of bread, vegetables and leafy salad greens, both meat and poultry play a welcome part in balanced and healthy main meal salads.

CHICKEN SALAD WITH CELERY, FRUIT AND ALMONDS

SERVES 2–3

A refreshing salad in which crisp crunchy vegetables and fruit contrast with tender chicken. Serve slightly chilled.

1 crisp red-skinned apple, unpeeled
lemon juice
1 small orange
275 g / 10 oz diced cooked chicken
4 tender celery stalks (from the centre of the bunch), leaves included, thinly sliced
40 g / 1½ oz toasted almonds with skin, halved lengthways
75 g / 3 oz Gruyère cheese, diced
½ tsp toasted cumin seeds
Creamy Herb Dressing (page 199)
salt and freshly ground black pepper
4–5 handfuls mixed salad greens, such as spinach, red oak lettuce and frisee, torn into bite-sized pieces
olive oil
fresh herb sprigs, to garnish

Quarter the apple and remove the core. Thinly slice crossways and put in a large bowl. Sprinkle with lemon juice to prevent browning.

Peel the orange and remove all the pith. Using a very sharp knife, thinly slice the flesh then cut into small segments. Add to the apples in the bowl together with the chicken, celery, almonds, cheese and cumin seeds. Stir in the dressing, toss gently and season to taste with salt and pepper. Chill for 30 minutes.

When ready to serve, toss the salad greens in a few drops of olive oil and arrange in a serving dish. Add the chicken mixture and garnish with herbs.

CHINESE CHICKEN SALAD WITH CRISPY RICE NOODLES

SERVES 3–4

This is just as delicious without the noodles, but they're fun to make. Before frying, pull the noodle threads apart and roughly break them into shorter lengths. Do this in a large deep bowl to stop them flying all over your kitchen.

3 boneless, skinless chicken breasts, about 150 g/5 oz each,
cut into 2 cm/¾ inch pieces
2 tbsp groundnut oil, plus more for deep-frying
100 g/4 oz mangetout, trimmed
50 g/2 oz thin rice noodles
½ head Chinese leaves, thinly sliced
3 spring onions, green parts included, sliced diagonally
40 g/1½ oz almonds with skins, sliced lengthways
Oriental Vinaigrette (page 189)

MARINADE
2 tbsp sugar
2 tbsp dry sherry
2 tsp shoyu
2 cm/¾ inch piece fresh ginger root
3 tbsp hoisin sauce
½ tsp salt
freshly ground black pepper

To make the marinade, dissolve the sugar in the sherry and shoyu. Crush the ginger root in a garlic press and add the juice to the mixture. Stir in the remaining ingredients.

Add the chicken, cover and marinade for at least 2 hours, or overnight. Drain the marinade.

Heat 2 tablespoons of groundnut oil in a pan or wok until almost smoking. Stir-fry the chicken for about 5 minutes until brown and crisp. Drain on paper towel and leave to cool.

Plunge the mangetout into a large pan of boiling water for 1 minute. Drain under cold running water, dry thoroughly and thinly slice diagonally.

Heat some more oil in a deep-fat fryer or saucepan until very hot. Add the noodles and remove them as soon as they puff up – this will take only a few seconds. Do not let them burn. Drain on paper towel.

Make a bed of Chinese leaves on a large shallow serving dish. Place the noodles in a pile on one side of the dish. Arrange the mangetout, onions, chicken and almonds in the remaining space and sprinkle with the vinaigrette. Serve at once.

CHICKEN AND AVOCADO SALAD WITH LIME AND CORIANDER

SERVES 2

A colourful, summery salad worth making in quantity for a party. The Coriander and Chilli Cream is really special.

2 boneless, skinless chicken breasts
Cumin and Lime Vinaigrette (page 190)
salt and freshly ground black pepper
1 avocado
3 handfuls mixed leaves (endive, escarole, rocket, young spinach,
lamb's lettuce), torn into bite-sized pieces
4 cherry tomatoes, halved
½ small yellow Roasted Pepper (page 178), diced
3 spring onions, green parts included, chopped
Coriander and Chilli Cream (page 200)
yellow or blue corn tortilla chips

Cut the chicken breasts in half lengthways and place between 2 sheets of polythene. Beat them with a rolling pin to a thickness of about 1.5 cm/½ inch. Slice in half lengthways again.

Place the chicken strips in a single layer in a shallow dish. Pour over enough vinaigrette to coat, then leave to marinate at room temperature for 20 minutes.

Heat a non-stick frying pan, add the chicken and the marinade, and season with salt and pepper. Fry for about 3 minutes each side until beginning to brown, then remove from the pan and set aside.

Halve the avocado and thinly slice crossways. Sprinkle with a little dressing to prevent discolouration.

Arrange the salad leaves on individual plates and scatter over the avocado, tomatoes, pepper and onions. Add a dollop of the coriander and chilli cream, with a few tortilla chips on the side for dipping.

Arrange the chicken strips on top and sprinkle with a little more dressing.

CHICKEN AND SORREL SALAD WITH CARROT, CUCUMBER AND KOHLRABI

SERVES 2

A cool and refreshing salad in which crisp crunchy matchstick vegetables contrast with tender chicken and sharp lemony sorrel. Supermarkets sometimes sell expensive little packets of sorrel, but it is very easy to grow, even in a pot on a window sill. Raw spinach, rocket or watercress would be good alternatives. If kohlrabi is unavailable, increase the amount of carrot and cucumber, or use celeriac instead.

1 small kohlrabi (weighing about 100 g/4 oz)
100 g/4 oz cucumber, unpeeled
1 carrot
2 handfuls sorrel
225 g/8 oz shredded cooked chicken
2 tbsp toasted sunflower seeds
Creamy Herb Dressing (page 199)

Peel the kohlrabi and slice thinly. Stack a few slices at a time, and cut into matchstick strips. Slice the cucumber and cut into matchstick strips in the same way. Cut the carrot into similar-sized matchstick strips.

Remove the sorrel stalks and shred the leaves finely. Do not use a knife, otherwise the leaves will bruise.

Put the chicken in a bowl and toss with the kohlrabi, cucumber, carrot and sorrel. Divide the mixture between individual plates and sprinkle with the sunflower seeds. Spoon the dressing over the salad and serve at once.

SESAME CHICKEN SALAD WITH GREEN AND RED PEPPERS

SERVES 2-3

This is fine on its own, but for extra substance you could serve it with some cold or warm cooked rice, bulgar wheat or noodles, tossed in a little shoyu and sesame oil.

1 tbsp toasted sesame seeds
2 tbsp light sesame oil
½ tsp toasted sesame oil
1 tbsp dry sherry
1 tbsp shoyu
1 garlic clove, finely chopped
salt and freshly ground black pepper
200 g/7 oz cooked chicken, diced
1 small red pepper, seeded and very thinly sliced
1 small green pepper, seeded and very thinly sliced
½ small red onion, very thinly sliced
75 g/3 oz can water chestnuts, drained and finely sliced
¼ head Chinese leaves, shredded

Combine the sesame seeds, oils, sherry, shoyu, garlic, and salt and pepper in a large bowl.

Add the chicken, peppers, onion and water chestnuts. Marinate for at least 1 hour.

Toss with the Chinese leaves just before serving.

CHICKEN TIKKA SALAD WITH GOLDEN RICE

SERVES 2–3

A brilliantly coloured salad, ideal for a summer barbecue. Marinate the chicken and cook the rice the day before you want to serve it. Serve with Coriander and Chilli Cream (page 200), Cucumber and Yogurt (page 167), or just plain yogurt.

*350 g / 12 oz boneless skinless chicken breasts, cut into
2.5 cm / 1 inch cubes
150 g / 5 oz long-grain brown rice
1 bay leaf
1 tsp ground turmeric
salt
5 tbsp olive oil
3 tbsp lime or lemon juice
2 tbsp chopped fresh flat-leafed parsley or coriander
1 tbsp snipped fresh chives
¼–½ tsp dried chilli flakes
freshly ground black pepper
3 tomatoes, seeded and chopped
2 tbsp finely chopped red onion
½ green pepper, seeded and diced
40 g / 1½ oz toasted cashew nuts
oil, for brushing
cos lettuce leaves, torn
coriander leaves, to garnish*

*MARINADE
125 ml / 4 fl oz plain yogurt
2 garlic cloves, crushed
2.5 cm / 1 inch piece fresh ginger root, crushed in a garlic press*

½ small onion, grated
1½ tsp chilli powder
1 tsp toasted coriander seeds, crushed
1 tsp ground cumin
½ tsp salt

Combine the marinade ingredients in a bowl. Add the chicken, turning to coat. Cover and marinate in the refrigerator for at least 6 hours or overnight.

Wash the rice and put in a saucepan with the bay leaf and enough water to cover by the depth of your thumbnail. Add the turmeric and ½ teaspoon of salt. Bring to the boil, stir once, then cover tightly and simmer over a very low heat for about 40 minutes until all the liquid is absorbed. Fluff with a fork and spread out in a dish to cool.

Whisk the oil, lime juice, parsley or coriander, chives, chilli flakes, and salt and pepper in a large bowl. Add the tomatoes, onion, green pepper and nuts. Carefully stir in the rice. Check the seasoning and add more oil or lemon juice if necessary.

Thread the chicken cubes onto skewers and brush with oil. Place under a preheated very hot grill or over coals. Grill for 8–10 minutes, turning and brushing with oil until cooked through.

When ready to serve, line a serving dish with cos lettuce and pile the rice mixture on top. Remove the chicken from the skewers and scatter over the rice. Garnish with coriander leaves.

CHICKEN WING, BACON AND MUSHROOM SALAD

SERVES 2–3

The chicken wings can be marinated and cooked a day ahead, but you could use any leftover barbecued meats, such as spare ribs or little lamb chops, instead of the wings.

600 g / 1¼ lb chicken wings
oil, for brushing
2 handfuls spinach, shredded
2–3 handfuls crisp lettuce, shredded
3 mushrooms, thinly sliced
½ red pepper, very thinly sliced
¼ small red onion, very thinly sliced
Balsamic Vinaigrette (page 187)
4–6 grilled bacon rashers, crumbled
Garlic Croutons (page 184) or Polenta Croutons (page 185)

MARINADE
3 tbsp reduced-sugar and salt tomato ketchup
2 tbsp hoisin sauce
2 tbsp clear honey
1 tbsp soy sauce
1 tbsp wine vinegar
1 tbsp Worcestershire sauce

Combine the marinade ingredients in a small bowl. Put the chicken wings in a single layer in a shallow dish. Pour over the marinade, turning to coat. Cover and leave to marinate in the refrigerator for at least 1 hour, but preferably overnight, turning occasionally.

When ready to cook, place on a rack under a preheated very

hot grill or over coals. Brush with oil. Grill for 15–20 minutes, turning and brushing with the marinade, until cooked through. Allow to cool slightly.

Put the spinach, lettuce, mushrooms, red pepper and onion in a shallow serving dish or on individual plates. Spoon over enough of the dressing to coat.

Top with the chicken wings and scatter over the bacon and croutons.

CHICKEN LIVER, BACON AND MANGETOUT SALAD WITH BITTER LEAVES

SERVES 2-3

This salad should be served warmish. It is quite filling but the bitter leaves counteract the richness of the livers. Unrefined roasted groundnut (peanut) oil adds that extra something, but you could use olive oil instead.

175 g/6 oz mangetout, trimmed
3 tbsp roasted groundnut (peanut) oil
2 tbsp balsamic vinegar
6 rashers streaky bacon, cut into small strips
sunflower oil, for frying
2 thick crustless slices bread, cubed
225 g/8 oz chicken livers, cleaned and chopped into small pieces
1 tsp dried oregano or thyme
salt and freshly ground black pepper
4–6 handfuls bitter leaves, such as escarole, curly endive, rocket and chicory, torn into bite-sized pieces

Plunge the mangetout into boiling water for 1 minute. Drain, cut in half crossways, and transfer to a bowl. Whisk the groundnut oil with 1 tablespoon of the vinegar and toss with the mangetout.

Fry the bacon strips in their own fat until crisp. Remove from the pan with a slotted spoon, drain on paper towel and keep warm.

Heat 5 tablespoons of sunflower oil in the same pan, and fry the bread cubes until golden on all sides. Drain on paper towel and add to the bacon. Add the chicken livers and oregano to the pan, and fry for 3 minutes until the livers are no longer pink, adding more oil if necessary. Season with salt and freshly ground black pepper. Stir in the remaining balsamic vinegar to deglaze the pan, and add to the bacon.

To serve, make a bed of salad leaves in a serving dish. Add the chicken liver mixture, and scatter over the mangetout. Sprinkle with groundnut oil left in the bowl.

BARBARY DUCK BREAST, WILD RICE AND BRAZIL NUT SALAD

SERVES 2–3

Barbary duck is beautifully tender and has more meat on the breast than ordinary duck. If you want to reduce the fat content, remove the skin after grilling. This salad will keep for two or three days and just gets better and better as the flavours develop. It is delicious served with a salad of pungent and bitter leaves, such as rocket, escarole, frisee and watercress.

2 Barbary duck breasts
salt
175 g/6 oz cooked wild rice (about 65 g/2½ oz uncooked)
175 g/6 oz cooked brown basmati rice (about 65 g/2½ oz uncooked)
1 carrot, shaved into ribbons
1 small courgette, coarsely grated
4 spring onions, green parts included, finely chopped
50 g/2 oz toasted Brazil nuts, roughly chopped
finely grated zest of ½ orange
2 tsp chopped fresh thyme or marjoram
Orange and Ginger Vinaigrette (page 193)
salt and freshly ground black pepper

Prick the skin of the duck breasts and rub with salt. Place under a preheated low-to-medium-hot grill for 10 minutes, skin side down in the grill pan (without a rack). Turn and grill for another 15 minutes, raising the heat towards the end to crisp the skin. Leave to stand for 10 minutes. Slice diagonally as thinly as possible, then cut into thin strips.

Put the rice in a bowl with the duck, carrot, courgette, spring onions, nuts, orange zest and thyme or marjoram. Pour over the dressing and toss gently. Season to taste with salt and freshly ground black pepper.

TURKEY AND PAPAYA SALAD WITH NUTS AND SPROUTED BEANS

SERVES 2–3

Turkey and densely fleshed fruit are an extremely good partnership, but this would be just as delicious made with grilled chicken or duck breasts; or peaches, nectarines or watermelon instead of papaya. Sprouted beans contain protein and B vitamins, and the papaya is rich in vitamins A and C.

75 g/3 oz mixed sprouted beans and alfafa sprouts
¼ head Chinese leaves, sliced lengthways and shredded
½ papaya, thinly sliced
1 kiwi fruit, thinly sliced
*175–225 g/6–8 oz cooked turkey breast, thinly sliced and cut
into strips*
40 g/1½ oz toasted cashew nuts
2 tbsp light olive oil
2 tbsp pistachio oil, or walnut oil
squeeze of lemon juice
salt and freshly ground black pepper

Toss together the sprouts and Chinese leaves in a shallow dish or on individual plates.

Arrange the papaya, kiwi fruit and turkey attractively on top. Scatter over the nuts.

Spoon over the oils, add a squeeze of lemon juice and season to taste.

WARM PIGEON SALAD WITH MANGETOUT, WALNUTS AND BACON

SERVES 2

Pigeon is quick and easy to prepare, and being low in fat is ideal for a healthy salad. It is also extremely rich in iron. Marinate the birds for as long as possible – overnight is best.

2 pigeons
1 tbsp raspberry vinegar
4 tbsp stock
salt
½ tbsp olive oil
50–75 g/2–3 oz piece smoked bacon, chopped
Grilled Polenta (page 185), cut into two 7.5 cm/3 inch squares
4 handfuls mixed bitter and pungent leaves, such as escarole, rocket,
lamb's lettuce, mustard greens, red oak lettuce
75 g/3 oz mangetout, trimmed and thinly sliced diagonally
25 g/1 oz toasted walnut halves

MARINADE
4 tbsp walnut oil
2 tbsp raspberry vinegar
2 garlic cloves, chopped
1 tsp black peppercorns, crushed
salt

Cut the pigeons into 4 (2 breasts and 2 legs), discarding the backbone. Put in a bowl with the marinade ingredients. Marinate for at least 1 hour, or overnight.

Put the pigeon breasts in a small roasting tin, reserving the marinade. Roast on the top shelf of a preheated oven at

240°C/475°F/gas 9 for 10 minutes. Add the legs and roast for another 7–8 minutes. The meat should still be pink inside. Leave in a warm place to rest for 10 minutes.

Pour the marinade into the roasting tin and place on top of the stove over a medium heat. Bring to the boil, scraping up any sediment from the bottom of the pan with a wooden spoon. Stir in the raspberry vinegar and stock. Simmer for a few minutes more, adding a little salt to taste. Keep warm.

Heat the olive oil in a small pan and fry the bacon until crisp. Remove and drain on paper towel.

Carve the pigeon breasts into thin slices, leave the legs whole.

Put a square of polenta in the centre of individual plates with the pigeon legs on top. Surround with the leaves. Scatter with the mangetout, bacon and walnuts. Add the pigeon breasts. Pour over the warmed marinade and serve at once.

DRY-CURED HAM AND AUBERGINE SALAD

SERVES 2

A quickly made salad full of robust flavours – pungent leaves, salty ham, rich aubergine and sweetly acidic tomato.

2 large handfuls escarole or frisee, torn into bite-sized pieces
1 handful trimmed rocket or watercress
4 slices dry-cured ham, such as prosciutto or serrano
4 tbsp ricotta cheese
1 tbsp toasted sunflower seeds
salt and freshly ground black pepper
½ head chicory, sliced lengthways
4 cherry tomatoes, halved
6–8 slices Oven-Dried Aubergine (page 177)
torn basil leaves, to garnish
extra virgin olive oil
few drops of balsamic vinegar

Arrange the escarole and rocket on individual plates, and top with the ham slices.

Mix the ricotta with the sunflower seeds and seasoning. Add a couple of spoonsful to each plate. Add the chicory, tomatoes and aubergine slices.

Sprinkle generously with basil, then drizzle with olive oil. Season to taste and sprinkle over a few drops of balsamic vinegar.

HAM AND PINK FIR APPLE POTATO SALAD

SERVES 2–3

A salad of beautiful shades of pink and orange. Use very thin slices of dry-cured ham such as Jambon de Bayonne or Italian prosciutto. Failing that, English cooked ham would do as long as it is wafer thin. Pink Fir Apple potatoes are an old breed with a wonderful earthy flavour. They are long and knobbly with a pink skin and a firm waxy texture – excellent for salads.

350 g/12 oz Pink Fir Apple potatoes, unpeeled
50 g/2 oz wafer thin slices dry-cured ham
2 spring onions
Marinated Carrot Ribbons (page 159)
6 radishes, sliced
Lemon Yogurt Dressing (page 198)
snipped fresh chives, to garnish

Boil the potatoes for 10–15 minutes until tender but still firm. Rinse under cold water, dry and cut into 5 mm/¼ inch slices.

Slice the ham into strips about the same width as the carrot ribbons.

Slice the onions into 4 lengthways, then cut into 2.5 cm/1 inch shreds.

Arrange the potato slices in a shallow serving dish, and drizzle with any juice from the carrots. Arrange the ham, carrot ribbons, spring onions and radishes on top.

Pour on the dressing, sprinkle with chives and serve.

HAM, COTTAGE CHEESE AND SUNFLOWER SEED SALAD

SERVES 2

Sunflower seeds and cottage cheese are a deliciously crunchy combination. Scoop up the mixture with the oatcakes. Eaten in reasonable amounts, sunflower seeds really boost the nutrients in salads. They're high in fat but contain no cholesterol. They're a good source of protein, vitamin E and folate, and are rich in minerals. For a lovely nutty flavour, dry-fry them in a heavy pan until they begin to colour.

150 g/5 oz cottage cheese
1 tbsp toasted sunflower seeds
2 tsp snipped fresh chives
2 thick slices cooked York ham
1 avocado, sliced crossways
¼ head Chinese leaves, sliced crossways
¼ cucumber, sliced thinly
3–4 tender celery stalks (from the centre of the bunch), sliced
6 cherry tomatoes
shoyu
extra virgin olive oil
oatcakes, to serve

Mix together the cottage cheese, sunflower seeds and chives.
Divide all the ingredients between individual plates, sprinkle with a few drops of shoyu and drizzle with olive oil. Serve with oatcakes.

PARMA HAM AND FENNEL SALAD

SERVES 2

This is a lively salad full of interesting bits and pieces – soft, sweet Parma ham, peppery watercress, crunchy fennel with its delicate hint of aniseed, topped with richly flavoured Parmesan wafers. Sea salt flakes and coarsely ground pepper add extra little bursts of flavour.

1 fennel bulb
juice of ½ lemon
3 tbsp extra virgin olive oil
2–3 handfuls trimmed watercress or rocket
4–6 thin slices Parma ham
2 oil-cured bottled artichokes, quartered
6 cherry tomatoes, halved
sea salt and coarsely ground black pepper
10 pitted black olives
Parmesan shavings
3 tbsp snipped fresh chives

Quarter the fennel bulb lengthways. Remove and discard the core. Slice lengthways into wafer-thin slivers. Put in a bowl and toss with the lemon juice and 2 tablespoons of the olive oil. Leave to stand for at least 30 minutes.

Arrange the watercress or rocket on a serving dish or individual plates. Place curls of Parma ham on top, and add the fennel, artichokes and tomatoes.

Season to taste with sea salt and a few grindings of black pepper. Scatter with the olives and a few Parmesan shavings. Sprinkle with chives and drizzle with the remaining olive oil.

SMOKED PORK AND RED CABBAGE SALAD WITH PISTACHIO NUTS

SERVES 2–3

Glistening red cabbage and brilliant green pistachio nuts are a stunning combination in an Eastern European-style salad.

25 g / 1 oz shelled pistachio nuts
250 g / 9 oz red cabbage, very thinly sliced
75 g / 3 oz piece smoked pork, finely diced
8 radishes, sliced
2 tsp chopped fresh dill or ½ tsp dill seeds
Balsamic Vinaigrette (page 187)
4–6 cooked new potatoes, sliced, to serve
4 cornichons (baby pickled cucumbers), to serve

Cover the pistachio nuts with boiling water and leave to soak for 5 minutes. Drain, then slip off the skins.

Put the red cabbage, pistachio nuts, pork and radishes in a serving bowl and toss with half the dill and enough dressing to coat.

Serve with the potatoes, sprinkled with a little more dressing and dill, and the cornichons.

PASTRAMI AND NEW POTATO SALAD

SERVES 2

Earthy new potatoes, tossed while still warm with crunchy sea salt, good olive oil and fresh herbs is my idea of heaven. Serve with good mustard and hot crusty bread.

350 g/12 oz small new potatoes, unpeeled
2 tbsp olive oil
coarse sea salt and coarsely ground black pepper
2 tbsp chopped mixed fresh herbs, such as lovage, chives, savory,
marjoram and thyme
6–8 thin slices pastrami
2 plum tomatoes, sliced
cos or Little Gem lettuce leaves, torn into bite-sized pieces

Boil the potatoes for about 10 minutes until just tender. Drain, return to the pan and immediately toss with the oil, sea salt, pepper and the herbs.

Arrange the pastrami on individual plates with the potatoes and the remaining ingredients. Drizzle with any oil and herbs remaining in the pan.

CHORIZO, CABBAGE, LENTIL AND CORIANDER SALAD

SERVES 2

This is a quickly made salad full of strong flavours. Use a good quality chorizo sausage and slice thinly. You could also add a one-egg omelette, rolled up and sliced into thin strips.

175 g/6 oz shredded white cabbage
75 g/3 oz thinly sliced chorizo sausage, cut into strips
2 plum tomatoes, seeded and chopped
100 g/4 oz cooked Puy lentils
5 tbsp chopped fresh coriander
Basic Vinaigrette (page 187)
salt and freshly ground black pepper

Combine the cabbage, chorizo, tomatoes, lentils and coriander in a bowl or on individual plates. Toss with the vinaigrette and season to taste.

SALAD OF ITALIAN CURED MEATS, TOMATO, ONION CONFIT AND GRILLED POLENTA

SERVES 2

Polenta is a mild-tasting grain with a deeply satisfying flavour. Cooked to a thick porridge, cooled and cut into shapes, then grilled until crisp, it can be used instead of croutons or potatoes and is ideal for mopping up tasty juices and dressings.

Grilled Polenta (page 185), cut into two 7.5 cm/3 inch squares
Tomato-Flavoured Red Onion Confit (page 176)
2 small rosemary sprigs
100 g/4 oz thinly sliced Italian cured meats, such as bresaola,
Milanese salami, coppa, Parma ham
2 plum tomatoes, thinly sliced
3 oil-cured bottled artichokes, quartered
pitted black olives
torn basil leaves
extra virgin olive oil
freshly ground black pepper

Place a polenta square in the centre of each plate with some onion confit and a rosemary sprig on top.

Arrange the meats and tomato slices round the edge. Scatter with the artichokes, olives and basil. Drizzle with olive oil and add a few grindings of black pepper.

MARINATED BEEF SALAD

SERVES 4

This is a gutsy salad, guaranteed to satisfy the most voracious of appetites. Use any kind of cooked beef – roasted or casseroled – and serve with warm crusty bread.

700 g / 1½ lb cooked beef, trimmed of fat and cut into
2 cm / ¾ inch cubes
2 shallots, finely chopped
2 tbsp capers, drained
4 tbsp chopped fresh flat-leafed parsley
3 tbsp snipped fresh chives
2 quantities Mustard Vinaigrette (page 189)
6 handfuls mixed salad greens
8 cooked new potatoes, sliced
4 tomatoes, peeled and sliced
4 hard-boiled eggs, sliced
pitted black olives, to garnish

Put the beef in a bowl and toss with the shallots, capers, 3 tablespoons of the parsley and 2 tablespoons of the chives. Pour over half the dressing and toss well. Cover and marinate for at least 2 hours or, better still, overnight.

When ready to serve, make a bed of salad leaves in a large serving dish or on individual plates. Arrange the potatoes, tomatoes and egg, on top. Spoon over some of the remaining dressing and sprinkle with the remaining parsley and chives.

Add the beef with the shallots and capers, and garnish with a few olives.

AIR-DRIED BEEF SALAD WITH SALSIFY AND MUSHROOMS

SERVES 2

Otherwise known as the oyster plant, salsify is a long thin tapered root with rough brown skin and creamy white flesh, in season from autumn to late spring. Salsify is sadly under-used in Britain, unlike the rest of Europe where it is enjoyed in salads and as a cooked vegetable. If you don't have any, use blanched celeriac or Jerusalem artichokes instead.

250 g/9 oz salsify, unpeeled
lemon juice
6 button mushrooms, thinly sliced
6 radishes, sliced
Horseradish and Lemon Dressing (page 199)
1 head radicchio, torn
handful of frisee
6–8 slices bresaola or Bündnerfleisch (air-dried beef), cut into strips
extra virgin olive oil
freshly ground black pepper
chopped fresh flat-leafed parsley, to garnish

Scrub the salsify and trim the ends. Boil for 30 minutes until just soft. Rub off the skins under cold running water, then pat dry with paper towel. Chop into 2.5 cm/1 inch pieces and sprinkle with lemon juice to prevent discolouration.

Mix the salsify, mushrooms and radishes with the horseradish dressing.

Put the radicchio leaves and frisee on individual plates with the bresaola or Bündnerfleisch on top. Sprinkle with a little olive oil and coarsely ground black pepper. Top with the salsify mixture and garnish with parsley.

SALAD OF GRILLED LAMB, BULGAR WHEAT, COURGETTE AND MINT

SERVES 4–6

Lamb seems to have a natural affinity with bulgar wheat and mint. It is a good source of iron and zinc, and the lean cuts are ideal for a robust main meal salad. Allow plenty of time for marinating. Serve the bulgur wheat at room temperature; the lamb can be still warm.

2 trimmed lamb fillets (from the loin end), about 275 g/10 oz each
225 g/8 oz bulgar wheat
2 tsp tomato purée
½ tsp salt
150 ml/¼ pint olive oil
juice of 1½ lemons
coarsely ground black pepper
½ red onion, finely diced
½ red pepper, finely diced
1 courgette, grated
handful of fresh mint leaves, coarsely chopped
3 handfuls mixed salad leaves
mint sprigs, to garnish
Minted Ratatouille (page 166), to serve

MARINADE
1½ tbsp olive oil
1½ tbsp safflower or sunflower oil
1 tbsp finely chopped fresh rosemary
1 tbsp fresh thyme
1 garlic clove, finely chopped
1 tsp coarsely ground black pepper

Combine the marinade oils and brush them all over the lamb. Combine the remaining marinade ingredients and rub them into the meat. Leave to marinate for at least 6 hours, turning occasionally. Allow to come to room temperature before grilling.

Meanwhile, wash the bulgar wheat in several changes of water until the water runs clear. Put in a saucepan with enough water to cover by 2 cm/¾ inch. Stir in the tomato purée and salt. Bring to the boil, cover and simmer over a very low heat until the liquid has been absorbed.

Transfer the bulgar wheat to a bowl, and gently stir in the olive oil, lemon juice and black pepper. Allow to cool.

Add the onion, red pepper, courgette and chopped mint. Toss gently and season to taste.

Place the meat on a rack under a preheated very hot grill. Sear all over, then reduce the heat and grill for 5 minutes each side. Allow to stand for 5 minutes then carve into slices.

Arrange the salad leaves in a shallow serving dish, and pile the bulgar wheat on top. Add the lamb slices and any juices. Garnish with mint sprigs and serve with the minted ratatouille.

SPICY LAMB SALAD WITH CARAMELISED ONION RINGS

SERVES 4–6

Allow the lamb to come to room temperature before grilling.
Serve warm or at room temperature.

12 small best end of neck lamb cutlets, trimmed of fat
oil, for brushing
Caramelised Onion Rings (page 175)
1 cos lettuce, trimmed and torn into bite-sized pieces
4 plum tomatoes, peeled and sliced
1 green pepper, seeded and thinly sliced
small bunch of radishes, sliced
pitted black olives
2 tbsp chopped fresh flat-leafed parsley
3–4 tbsp extra virgin olive oil
salt and freshly ground black pepper
Cucumber and Yogurt (page 167), to serve

MARINADE
1 tsp toasted coriander seeds
1 tsp toasted cumin seeds
seeds from 2 cardamom pods
½ tsp black peppercorns
2 tbsp chopped fresh mint
½ tsp coarse sea salt
3 garlic cloves, finely chopped
1 tbsp harissa
150 ml/¼ pint Greek yogurt

To make the marinade, coarsely crush the spices and mint with
the salt. Mix with the garlic, harissa and yogurt. Rub the

mixture over the lamb and leave to marinate for at least 1 hour or preferably overnight.

Brush the chops with oil and place on a rack with the onion rings under a preheated very hot grill or over hot coals. Grill for 5–7 minutes each side or until beginning to blacken round the edges.

Put the salad ingredients in a shallow serving dish and toss with the parsley, olive oil and seasoning. Arrange the lamb and the onion rings on top. Spoon over some of the cucumber and yogurt and serve the rest in a bowl.

WARM LENTIL AND RABBIT SALAD WITH LOVAGE, WALNUTS AND GREEN PEPPERCORNS

SERVES 2–3

Lovage has an almost indescribable warm flavour, reminiscent of curry and celery. If you haven't got any, add a pinch of curry powder or ground fenugreek to the lentils and use chopped celery leaves or flat-leafed parsley instead.

4 boneless rabbit joints
1 tbsp olive oil
½ red onion, very finely diced
1 celery stalk, very finely diced
1 garlic clove, finely chopped
175 g / 6 oz Puy lentils, washed and drained
3 tbsp chopped fresh lovage
salt
600 ml / 1 pint stock
40 g / 1½ oz toasted walnuts, roughly chopped
Walnut and Green Peppercorn Dressing (page 196)
6 handfuls lamb's lettuce
175 g / 6 oz cherry tomatoes, halved

MARINADE
4 tbsp olive oil
juice of 1 lemon
1 garlic clove, crushed
1 tsp green peppercorns, crushed

Slash the thickest parts of the rabbit joints with a sharp knife to allow the marinade to penetrate further. Combine the marinade ingredients and pour over the rabbit, turning to coat.

Marinate for at least 2 hours or preferably overnight.

Place the rabbit under a preheated hot grill, and grill for 15–20 minutes, until slightly blackened, turning regularly and brushing with the marinade. Slice thinly and set aside.

Heat the oil in a saucepan and gently fry the onion and celery for 2 minutes until translucent. Add the garlic and fry for another minute. Stir in the lentils, 2 tablespoons of the lovage, and season with salt. Add the stock, bring to the boil and simmer for 20 minutes, until the lentils are just tender. Drain off any excess liquid.

Toss the lentils with the rabbit, two-thirds of the walnuts and two-thirds of the dressing while still warm. Check the seasoning.

Make a bed of lamb's lettuce on a serving dish or individual plates. Pile the lentils and rabbit in the centre, with the tomatoes round the edge. Sprinkle with the remaining walnuts and lovage. Drizzle with the remaining dressing and serve at once.

FRANKFURTER AND POTATO SALAD

SERVES 2–3

A very quickly made salad. It is particularly delicious when the frankfurters are still warm. The caraway seeds are not essential so leave them out if you grew up hating seed cake!

275 g / 10 oz frankfurters, cut into 2.5 cm / 1 inch pieces
2 hard-boiled eggs, roughly chopped
4 cooked new potatoes, cut into chunks
2 tbsp finely chopped onion
½ green pepper, diced
10 radishes, sliced
½ tsp caraway seeds
Creamy Herb Dressing (page 199), made with plenty of fresh dill
salt and freshly ground black pepper

Put the frankfurters and eggs in a bowl with the potatoes, onion, pepper, radishes and caraway seeds. Toss with enough dressing to coat and season to taste.

4

Salads with Cheese

A good slice of cheese in peak condition transforms a light and leafy salad into a nutritionally balanced main meal. Outstanding in their number and variety, cheeses have a great affinity with leafy greens, they go well with onions, olives and pickles, and add sharpness and flavour to root vegetable salads.

As well as protein, cheeses provide useful amounts of vitamins A and E, calcium and zinc. Hard and semi-hard cheeses, such as Parmesan, Cheddar or Emmenthal, have an undeniably high fat content. But with their intense flavour, a little goes a long way to adding depth and richness to a main meal salad.

EMMENTHAL, SPINACH AND ROASTED PEPPER SALAD

SERVES 2

A colourful quickly made salad, rich in carotene (vitamin A), potassium, calcium, iron and folate. Slicing the cheese into thin wafers brings out the full flavour.

75 g/3 oz Emmenthal cheese
4 handfuls young spinach, trimmed and torn into bite-sized pieces
½ red Roasted Pepper (page 178), diced
Garlic Croutons (page 184)
1 tbsp chopped fresh chives
Walnut Vinaigrette (page 188)

Using a swivel peeler, shave the cheese into thin wafers.

Put all the ingredients in a serving bowl or arrange on individual plates. Toss with the dressing and serve at once.

Roasted Vegetable Salad*(page 8)*

Californian Salad Platter *(page 29)* **with Guacamole** *(page 174)*

Smoked Salmon, Prawn, Asparagus and Watercress Salad *(page 63)*
with Potato Salad with Yogurt and Mint *(page 165)*

**Chicken and Sorrel Salad with Carrot,
Cucumber and Kohlrabi** *(page 72)*

Salad of Italian Cured Meats, Tomato, Onion Confit and Grilled Polenta *(page 91)*

Feta Salad with Broad Beans and Mint (*page 108*)

Warm Goat's Cheese and Cabbage Salad with Pumpkin Seeds and Nasturtiums *(page 111)*

Kidney Bean and Avocado Salad with Two Sauces *(page 130)*
with Smoked Sweetcorn and Chilli Salsa *(page 171)*

WENSLEYDALE, PEAR AND GREEN BEAN SALAD

SERVES 2

The green peppercorns in the dressing add a mysterious smoky flavour which is delicious with the pears.

1 juicy red-skinned pear, unpeeled
lemon juice
100 g/4 oz cooked green beans, cut into 2 cm/¾ inch pieces
4 tender celery stalks, thinly sliced diagonally
1 tbsp chopped fresh flat-leafed parsley
Walnut and Green Peppercorn Dressing (page 196)
freshly ground black pepper
1 head red chicory, cut lengthways into thin slivers
4 handfuls trimmed rocket
50 g/2 oz Wensleydale cheese, crumbled

Quarter the pear and remove the core. Cut crossways into thin slices. Sprinkle with lemon juice to prevent browning. Put in a bowl with the beans, celery and parsley, and toss with enough of the dressing to coat. Season with pepper.

Toss the chicory and rocket in a little dressing. Arrange in a serving dish or on individual plates. Add the pear mixture and scatter with the cheese.

MEXICAN CHEESE SALAD

SERVES 2

The Smoked Sweetcorn and Chilli Salsa (page 171) would be good to serve with this. You could also add a few cooked kidney beans for a really substantial salad.

4 handfuls shredded iceberg or cos lettuce
1 avocado, halved and peeled
1 green pepper, diced
½ small red onion, thinly sliced
2 tomatoes, chopped
1 small green chilli, seeded and finely diced
Lime and Coriander Dressing (page 198)
50 g/2 oz Cheddar cheese, coarsely grated
4 tbsp soured cream, or Coriander and Chilli Cream (page 200)
coriander leaves, to garnish

Put the lettuce on individual plates. Place the avocado on top, cut side down and cut crossways into thin slices. Scatter the pepper, onion, tomatoes and chilli around the edge.

Sprinkle with the dressing. Add the cheese and top the avocado with the soured cream or the coriander and chilli cream. Garnish with coriander leaves.

ROQUEFORT AND WALNUT SALAD

SERVES 2

Crisp and crunchy, the new season's 'wet' walnuts are best of all. Otherwise, toast ordinary walnuts in the oven to bring out the flavour. Although high in fat, walnuts are a very good source of protein, potassium, iron, zinc, B vitamins and vitamin E. They also contain selenium, an important trace mineral thought to inhibit cancer and help protect from heart disease.

2 handfuls each butterhead lettuce, frisee and rocket
150 g/5 oz Roquefort cheese, crumbled
40 g/1½ oz walnut halves
4 small tender celery stalks (from the centre of the bunch), sliced
2–3 cooked new potatoes, sliced
1 tbsp snipped fresh chives
Walnut Vinaigrette (page 188)

Put the salad greens in a bowl with the cheese, walnuts, celery, potatoes and chives. Pour the dressing over the salad and toss gently. The leaves should be just coated with oil.

BLUE CHEESE, TOMATO, CELERY AND LENTIL SALAD

SERVES 2–3

Use a crumbly blue cheese such as Bleu d'Auvergne, Stilton or Roquefort. Let the salad stand at room temperature for at least an hour to allow the flavours to develop. Good served with a simple salad of rocket or watercress tossed in a little olive oil.

175 g/6 oz Puy lentils
1½ tbsp white wine vinegar
1 garlic clove, finely chopped
2 tsp finely chopped fresh rosemary
salt and freshly ground black pepper
3 tbsp extra virgin olive oil
4 tender celery stalks (from the middle of the bunch), diced
6 cherry tomatoes, quartered
100 g/4 oz blue cheese, crumbled
3 grilled bacon rashers, crumbled
chopped celery leaves, to garnish

Rinse the lentils and put in a saucepan with 350 ml/12 fl oz water. Bring to the boil, then cover and simmer over a very low heat for 20–25 minutes until just tender. Drain off any excess liquid.

Combine the vinegar, garlic, rosemary and seasoning in a small bowl, then whisk in the oil. Pour the mixture over the lentils while they are still warm.

Toss with the remaining ingredients and leave to stand for at least 1 hour. Garnish with celery leaves before serving.

BLUE CHEESE, RADICCHIO, ORANGE AND FENNEL SALAD

SERVES 2

A beautiful salad with jewel-like colours and contrasting flavours of walnuts and citrus fruit.

1 small orange
1 fennel bulb
1 head radicchio, torn into bite-sized pieces
100 g/4 oz blue cheese, crumbled
25 g/1 oz toasted walnut halves
torn basil leaves
Walnut Citrus Dressing (page 195)

Peel the orange and remove the pith and seeds. Using a very sharp knife, thinly slice horizontally and cut into small segments.

Trim the fennel and cut into 4 lengthways. Remove the core, then slice vertically into thin slithers.

Arrange the radicchio in a shallow serving dish or on individual plates. Scatter over the orange and fennel, and top with the cheese, walnuts and basil. Drizzle with the dressing.

FETA SALAD WITH BROAD BEANS AND MINT

SERVES 2

Milk-white crumbled feta cheese looks beautiful against cool greens, red tomatoes and black olives. You will not need any extra salt because of the saltiness of the cheese and the olives.

175 g/6 oz frozen or fresh shelled broad beans
3 tomatoes, seeded and chopped
1 green pepper, diced
20 pitted black olives
large handful each of cos and red oak lettuce, torn into bite-sized pieces
150 g/5 oz feta cheese, crumbled
3 tbsp chopped fresh mint
juice of ½ lemon
4 tbsp extra virgin olive oil
freshly ground black pepper

Plunge the beans into plenty of boiling water for 2 minutes. Drain under cold running water. Slip off the outer skins if they are tough.

Put all the ingredients in a shallow serving dish and toss with the lemon juice, olive oil and a few grindings of black pepper.

SALAD OF FETA CHEESE, BROAD BEANS, CABBAGE, KOHLRABI AND PUMPKIN SEEDS

SERVES 2–3

A beautiful salad of white and different shades of green, with lively herbs. Pumpkin seed oil is a very special oil which is reflected in the price. If you don't have any, use the Basic Vinaigrette (page 187) instead. Or replace the pumpkin seeds with walnuts and use Walnut Vinaigrette (page 188).

1 small kohlrabi (weighing about 100 g/4 oz)
75 g/3 oz shredded green cabbage
100 g/4 oz cooked broad beans, or flageolot beans
1 green pepper, diced
4 spring onions, green parts included, sliced
1 tbsp snipped fresh chives
1 tbsp chopped fresh mint
1 tbsp chopped fresh coriander
2 tbsp toasted pumpkin seeds
Pumpkin Seed Vinaigrette (page 192)
100 g/4 oz feta cheese, crumbled
pitted black olives, to garnish

Peel and thinly slice the kohlrabi. Stack a few slices at a time and cut into matchstick strips.

Put the kohlrabi in a salad bowl with the cabbage, beans, green pepper, onions, herbs and two-thirds of the pumpkin seeds.

Toss with the vinaigrette. Sprinkle over the feta cheese and remaining pumpkin seeds, and garnish with olives.

GOAT'S CHEESE, BEETROOT, ROCKET AND MINT SALAD

SERVES 2–3

A richly coloured salad of raw grated beetroot with lots of garlic and mint on a bed of peppery rocket. Add the beetroot immediately before serving and position it exactly where you want it, otherwise the salad will be swimming with red juice.

2 tbsp lemon juice
1 garlic clove, finely chopped
4 tbsp extra virgin olive oil
salt and freshly ground black pepper
3 small uncooked beetroot, peeled and coarsely grated
2 spring onions, green parts included, finely chopped
5 tbsp chopped fresh mint
5–6 handfuls trimmed rocket
100 g / 4 oz goat's cheese, crumbled
25 g / 1 oz toasted walnuts, roughly chopped
mint sprigs, to garnish

Whisk the lemon juice, garlic, oil, and salt and pepper.

Put the beetroot in a bowl with the spring onions, 1 tablespoon of the chopped mint and 3 tablespoons of the dressing. Season to taste.

Arrange the rocket on individual plates and sprinkle with the remaining mint. Drizzle with a little of the dressing.

Put the beetroot mixture in the middle. Scatter over the goat's cheese and walnuts and garnish with a mint sprig.

WARM GOAT'S CHEESE AND CABBAGE SALAD WITH PUMPKIN SEEDS AND NASTURTIUMS

SERVES 2

The nasturtiums are not essential but they look beautiful and they add a lovely pepper flavour to the salad. You could use watercress or rocket instead. If you don't have pumpkin seed oil, use walnut oil or extra virgin olive oil instead.

75 g/3 oz finely shredded green cabbage
75 g/3 oz finely shredded white cabbage
2 small carrots, thinly sliced
½ green pepper, diced
nasturtium leaves
1 tbsp toasted pumpkin seeds
pumpkin seed oil
squeeze of lemon juice
coarse sea salt and freshly ground black pepper
150 g/5 oz goat's cheese log, halved horizontally
nasturtium petals, to garnish

Combine the cabbages, carrots, green pepper, a few nasturtium leaves and the pumpkin seeds. Divide between individual plates. Drizzle with pumpkin seed oil and a squeeze of lemon, and season to taste.

Place the cheese under a preheated hot grill for 1–2 minutes until slightly softened and beginning to colour. Using a fish slice, place the cheese on top of the salad and garnish with nasturtium petals. Serve at once.

SALAD OF GOAT'S CHEESE, GRILLED AUBERGINES AND COURGETTES WITH POLENTA CROUTONS

SERVES 2

This may seem a bit fiddly but it is easier than it sounds and the end result is absolutely delicious. You could use cubes of mozzarella instead of goat's cheese.

1 large courgette
1 aubergine
olive oil, for brushing
freshly ground black pepper
4 large basil leaves, roughly torn
50 g/2 oz goat's cheese
1 Little Gem lettuce
2 handfuls rocket
6 cherry tomatoes, halved
hazelnut oil
lemon juice
Polenta Croutons (page 185)
basil leaves, to garnish

Cut away and discard the skin from opposite sides of the courgette and the aubergine. Slice the remaining straight-edged part lengthways, so you end up with four 1 cm/½ inch thick slices of each. Lightly brush with oil on both sides and season with pepper. Place under a preheated very hot grill and grill for 2–3 minutes until just beginning to colour. Allow to cool.

Lay the slices flat and top each with pieces of basil leaf. Place a teaspoonful of goat's cheese at one end and roll up tightly. Place seam sides down on an oiled baking sheet. Place under a very hot grill for 4–6 minutes until golden brown.

Arrange the salad leaves and tomatoes on individual plates. Sprinkle with a little hazelnut oil and a squeeze of lemon juice. Add the aubergine and courgette rolls, top with the basil leaves and scatter over the polenta croutons. Serve at once.

WARM GOAT'S CHEESE SALAD WITH ONION CONFIT AND FENNEL

SERVES 2

A zesty salad of contrasting flavours and textures – soft, salty goat's cheese, sweet buttery onion and crisp garlic-flavoured breadcrumbs. Goat's cheese contains vitamins D, E, and B complex, and only a moderate amount of fat.

4 handfuls pungent salad greens, such as frisee, young dandelion leaves, escarole, land cress
2 oil-cured sun-dried tomatoes, cut into strips
75 g/3 oz Tomato-Flavoured Red Onion Confit
(page 176)
½ fennel bulb, cored and thinly sliced
12–14 pitted black olives
2 tsp lemon juice
3 tbsp extra virgin olive oil
salt and freshly ground black pepper
2 tbsp light olive oil
25 g/1 oz wholemeal breadcrumbs
½ tsp dried oregano or thyme
1 garlic clove, finely chopped
2 × 2 cm/¾ inch slices firm goat's cheese

Arrange the salad greens on a serving dish or individual plates. Scatter with the sun-dried tomato, sliced onion confit, fennel and olives. Sprinkle with the lemon juice and extra virgin olive oil, and season to taste.

Heat the light olive oil in a pan and fry the breadcrumbs and oregano for 2 minutes until golden, adding the garlic halfway through.

Place the cheese slices under a preheated very hot grill for 2–3 minutes, until just beginning to melt. Using a fish slice, place the cheese on top of the salad and sprinkle with the breadcrumbs. Serve at once.

GOAT'S CHEESE AND BROAD BEAN SALAD WITH OVEN-DRIED TOMATOES AND AUBERGINES

SERVES 2

If you don't have oven-dried tomatoes to hand, use 3 large plum tomatoes with a good flavour and sprinkle them with a little chopped garlic, sea salt and freshly ground black pepper.

150g/5 oz dry goat's cheese
1 small Roasted Chilli (page 182), finely diced, or 1 tsp dried chilli
flakes
1 tbsp toasted sesame seeds
freshly ground black pepper
4 tbsp chopped fresh coriander
175 g/6 oz shelled fresh or frozen broad beans
½ tsp kalonji seeds (onion seeds), or black cumin seeds
2 tbsp light sesame oil or unrefined safflower oil
½ quantity Oven-Dried Tomatoes (page 157)
½ Oven-Dried Aubergine (page 177)

Put the goat's cheese in a bowl and mix with the chilli, sesame seeds, pepper and half the coriander. Form into walnut-sized balls and roll in the remaining coriander. Carefully put them on a plate and chill for 30 minutes.

Plunge the beans into plenty of boiling water for 2–3 minutes. Drain, return to the pan and add the kalonji seeds and the sesame oil. Place over a very low heat until the oil has warmed through.

Place the tomatoes in the centre of individual plates. Arrange the beans and aubergine slices around the edge and pour over the warmed oil. Season to taste with salt and pepper. Place the goat's cheese on top and serve at once.

MOZZARELLA AND MEDITERRANEAN VEGETABLE SALAD

SERVES 2

You could use any combination of roasted vegetables – these are only suggestions. Or you could use bottled vegetables such as red and yellow peppers, mushrooms, aubergines or oil-cured sun-dried tomatoes.

175 g/6 oz Italian mozzarella cheese (preferably buffalo milk),
thinly sliced
1 large plum tomato, thinly sliced
coarse sea salt and freshly ground black pepper
extra virgin olive oil
torn basil leaves
1 head radicchio, vertically sliced into eighths
2 handfuls trimmed rocket
2 oil-cured bottled artichoke hearts, quartered
1 Oven-Dried Aubergine (page 177)
1 red Roasted Pepper (page 178), thinly sliced
1 Roasted Courgette (page 180), cut into chunks
pitted black olives, to garnish

Make a circle of overlapping cheese and tomato slices in the centre of individual plates. Season generously with salt and pepper, drizzle with olive oil and sprinkle with basil leaves.

Toss the radicchio and rocket in a drop of olive oil – just enough to barely coat the leaves. Arrange round the cheese and tomatoes.

Scatter the artichokes, aubergine, pepper and courgette over the leaves. Garnish with a few black olives and serve at once.

GRUYERE, GREEN BEAN AND HAM SALAD

SERVES 2

Gruyère is very rich in calcium but it is also high in fat. If you're trying to reduce your fat intake, use a reduced-fat Edam instead. It doesn't have the same intense flavour, but it would be a reasonable substitute.

1 shallot, finely chopped
1 garlic clove, finely chopped
1 tbsp red wine vinegar
1 tbsp grainy mustard
salt and freshly ground black pepper
3 tbsp extra virgin olive oil
175 g / 6 oz Gruyère cheese
175 g / 6 oz cooked green beans, cut into 2 cm / ¾ inch pieces
175 g / 6 oz air-dried ham, cut into strips
2 handfuls trimmed young spinach, shredded
4 spring onions, sliced
6 radishes, sliced
½ tsp dill seeds
Garlic Croutons (page 184)

Combine the shallot, garlic, vinegar, mustard, and salt and pepper in a serving bowl. Add the oil and whisk until thick.

Using a swivel peeler, shave the cheese into very thin strips. Add to the bowl with the remaining ingredients.

Toss to mix and serve at once.

CAESAR SALAD

SERVES 2–3

A classic salad which usually contains raw egg. I have omitted it in order to reduce the cholesterol content. Make sure you use really crisp cos lettuce. Discard the outer leaves and use the inner leaves only. Go easy on the salt if you add anchovies.

1½ tbsp lemon juice
2 tsp Dijon mustard
1 garlic clove, finely chopped
dash of Worcestershire sauce
salt
¼ tsp freshly ground black pepper
75 ml / 3 fl oz extra virgin olive oil
1–2 cos lettuces, inner leaves only
3 anchovies (optional), chopped
40 g / 1½ oz Parmesan cheese, coarsely grated
warm Garlic Croutons (page 184)

Mix together the lemon juice, mustard, garlic, Worcestershire sauce, and salt and pepper. Gradually add the oil and whisk until thick.

Tear the lettuce into bite-sized pieces and place in a salad bowl with the anchovies and half the Parmesan. Pour the dressing over the leaves and toss well. Sprinkle with the remaining cheese and scatter with a handful of warm croutons. Serve immediately.

PECORINO, PEAR, CELERY AND WATERCRESS SALAD

SERVES 2

Choose ripe, juicy pears such as Forelle or Williams.

2 pears, unpeeled
juice of 1 lemon
4 tender celery stalks with leaves (from the centre of the bunch)
1½ tbsp toasted pumpkin seeds
4 handfuls trimmed watercress
50 g/2 oz pecorino or Parmesan cheese, shaved into wafers
extra virgin olive oil
coarsely ground black pepper
pumpkin seed oil

Quarter and core the pears, then cut lengthways into thin slices. Put in a salad bowl and sprinkle with the lemon juice to prevent browning.

Cut the celery into thin diagonal slices, leaving the leaves intact, and add to the pears. Add 1 tablespoon of the pumpkin seeds, the watercress and cheese. Toss with enough olive oil to barely coat the leaves.

Add a few grindings of black pepper and the remaining pumpkin seeds, and drizzle with a little pumpkin seed oil.

SMOKED CHEESE, APPLE, CHICORY AND WATERCRESS SALAD

SERVES 2

The combination of flavour and texture of crisp apples, walnuts and salty smoked cheese is irresistible. If you don't have smoked cheese, use Wensleydale or Roquefort.

1 crisp red-skinned apple, unpeeled
lemon juice
175 g/6 oz smoked cheese, very thinly sliced
40 g/1½ oz toasted walnuts, roughly chopped
2 tbsp snipped fresh chives
2 heads chicory
2–3 handfuls trimmed watercress
walnut oil
sea salt and coarsely ground black pepper

Core and thinly slice the apple. Sprinkle with lemon juice to prevent browning. Mix with the cheese, walnuts and chives.

Quarter the chicory lengthways and separate the leaves. Arrange round the edge of individual plates and scatter with the watercress. Top with the apple and cheese mixture.

Sprinkle with more lemon juice and drizzle with walnut oil. Add a little sea salt and a few grindings of black pepper. Serve at once.

5

Salads with Pulses, Grains and Noodles

The strong full flavours of olives, garlic, chillies, onions, pickles, cheeses and meats add untold depths to these comforting, filling salads. Crisp cooked or raw vegetables and nuts contrast well with the soft starchy texture of cooked beans and grains.

Although they may take longer to prepare, these salads can be made ahead of time. They positively benefit from being allowed to stand at room temperature for a while, and they can also be kept in the fridge for several days.

CHILLIED BLACK BEAN SALAD WITH RED AND YELLOW PEPPERS

SERVES 2–3

Serve this with Guacamole (page 174), or add an avocado, diced and tossed in lime juice, just before serving.

150 g/5 oz black turtle beans, soaked overnight
salt
Lime and Coriander Dressing (page 198)
2 tsp toasted cumin seeds
freshly ground black pepper
4 spring onions, green parts included, very finely sliced
1 red pepper, seeded and finely diced
1 yellow pepper, seeded and finely diced
1 fresh red or green chilli, seeded and very finely chopped
1 tbsp chopped fresh coriander, to garnish
tortillas or taco shells, to serve

Drain the beans and put in a saucepan with enough water to cover. Bring to the boil and boil rapidly for 20 minutes. Cook for a little longer until just tender, adding salt during the last 10 minutes of cooking. Drain and put in a serving bowl.

Pour the dressing over the beans while still warm. Toss with the cumin seeds and seasoning. Allow to cool.

Stir in the onions, peppers and chilli, adding more oil or lime juice if necessary. Allow to stand at room temperature for at least 1 hour. Garnish with coriander and serve with warmed tortillas or taco shells.

BLACK BEAN, PALM HEART AND PAN-SMOKED SWEETCORN SALAD

SERVES 2-3

Palm hearts are the buds of a West Indian palm tree. Sold in cans, they have a lovely squeaky crunchy texture with a flavour similar to artichoke hearts. Unused palm hearts can be covered with water and kept in the fridge for a day or two. Slice them thinly and add to tomato or green salads.

175g/6 oz black turtle beans, soaked overnight
salt
Cumin and Lime Vinaigrette (page 190)
2 sweetcorn ears
½ tsp coarse sea salt
100 g/4 oz drained canned palm hearts
½ green pepper, seeded and finely diced
2 tbsp chopped fresh flat-leafed parsley
½ tsp dried chilli flakes
freshly ground black pepper

Boil the beans rapidly in unsalted water for 20 minutes, then continue to cook for a little longer until just soft, adding salt in the last 10 minutes of cooking time. Drain and toss with some of the dressing while still warm.

Cut the kernels off the sweetcorn ears and mix with the sea salt. Heat a heavy-based iron frying pan (not a non-stick one) until very hot. Add the kernels, leave for a few seconds, then scrape them up and stir them around the pan. Repeat this 3 or 4 times until the kernels are slightly blackened. Add to the beans.

Cut the palm hearts lengthways into 4, then slice crossways

into 1.5 cm/½ inch pieces. Add to the beans together with the remaining ingredients.

Allow to stand at room temperature for at least 1 hour before serving.

SALAD OF PINK AND GREEN BEANS WITH KOHLRABI, GREEN PEPPER AND PUMPKIN SEEDS

SERVES 3–4

The cooking time depends on the age of the beans. The borlotti beans will take longer than the flageolet beans. If you don't have these, use any two beans of contrasting colour such as haricot and red kidney beans.

100 g/4 oz flageolet beans, soaked overnight
100 g/4 oz borlotti beans, soaked overnight
salt
½ tsp Dijon mustard
Pumpkin Seed Vinaigrette (page 192), or Basic Vinaigrette (page 187)
4 tbsp chopped fresh flat-leafed parsley
3 tbsp pumpkin seeds
2 spring onions, chopped
freshly ground black pepper
4 handfuls bitter and pungent green leaves, such as frisee, escarole, rocket, red oak
2 small kohlrabi, peeled and cut into matchstick strips
1 green pepper, seeded and cut into matchstick strips
2 hard-boiled eggs, chopped

Drain the beans and put in separate saucepans. Cover with water and bring to the boil. Boil briskly for 20 minutes, then continue to cook until just tender, adding salt during the last 10 minutes of cooking.

Drain the beans and mix together in a bowl. Add the

mustard to the vinaigrette and whisk until thick. Pour all but 2 tablespoons over the beans while they are still warm. Leave to cool, then stir in 3 tablespoons of the parsley, 2 tablespoons of the pumpkin seeds and the spring onions. Season to taste.

Arrange the leaves on individual plates or round the edge of a serving dish. Pile the beans in the middle with the kohlrabi, pepper and eggs on top. Sprinkle with the remaining pumpkin seeds, parsley and dressing.

BLACK AND WHITE BEAN SALAD

SERVES 2–3

For a really colourful presentation and a great taste sensation, serve this with Guacamole (page 174) and a few mixed salad leaves. Allow to stand at room temperature for at least 1 hour before serving. It will keep in the fridge for a few days.

100 g / 4 oz black turtle beans, soaked overnight
100 g / 4 oz haricot beans, soaked overnight
2 bay leaves
salt
Cumin and Lime Vinaigrette (page 190)
freshly ground black pepper
2 red peppers, seeded and diced
1 fresh red chilli, seeded and finely chopped
2 white cocktail onions, thinly sliced
3–4 pieces oil-cured sun-dried tomatoes, diced, or 1 tbsp dried tomato flakes
10 pitted black olives
chopped fresh coriander, to garnish

Put the beans in separate saucepans each with a bay leaf. Cover with water, bring to the boil and boil rapidly for 20 minutes. Continue to cook if necessary, until just soft, adding salt during the last 10 minutes of cooking time. Drain and toss with the vinaigrette while still warm. Season to taste.

Allow to cool then stir in the remaining ingredients and garnish with coriander.

KIDNEY BEAN AND CABBAGE SALAD WITH DILL AND HAZELNUTS

SERVES 2–3

This is delicious served with cottage cheese mixed with chopped fresh dill and some toasted sunflower seeds. Although high in fat, hazelnuts are extremely rich in vitamin E, potassium, iron and folate.

75 g/3 oz kidney beans, soaked overnight
salt
Hazelnut Vinaigrette (page 188)
freshly ground black pepper
1 tbsp each chopped fresh dill and chives
50 g/2 oz thinly shredded white cabbage
50 g/2 oz thinly shredded red cabbage
1 celery stalk, sliced diagonally
1 carrot, coarsely grated
40 g/1½ oz toasted hazelnuts, roughly chopped

Put the kidney beans in a saucepan and cover with plenty of water. Bring to the boil and boil rapidly for 20 minutes, then continue to cook until just tender. This could take anything from 15–30 minutes. Add salt during the last 10 minutes of cooking.

Drain and toss with some of the dressing while still warm. Season to taste and allow to cool.

Stir in the other ingredients and toss with the remaining dressing, adding more oil and seasoning if necessary.

KIDNEY BEAN AND AVOCADO SALAD WITH TWO SAUCES

SERVES 2–3

A colourful, gutsy salad with a Mexican feel, worth making in quantity for a party. It's fine as it is, but you could serve it with some warmed tortillas and Smoked Sweetcorn and Chilli Salsa (page 171), or Tomato and Cucumber Salsa (page 169).

150 g/5 oz kidney beans, soaked overnight
salt
4 tbsp extra virgin olive oil
3 spring onions, finely chopped
2 tbsp chopped fresh parsley
6 tbsp Roasted Pepper and Yogurt Sauce (page 201)
freshly ground black pepper
2 avocados
1 tbsp lime juice
2 Little Gem lettuces
1 head chicory
½ yellow pepper, seeded and finely diced
2 plum tomatoes, halved and thinly sliced
Coriander and Chilli Cream (page 200)
chopped fresh coriander or flat-leafed parsley, to garnish

Drain and rinse the kidney beans, and put in a saucepan with plenty of water. Bring to the boil and boil rapidly for 20 minutes then continue to cook until just tender. This could take anything from 15–30 minutes. Add salt during the last 10 minutes of cooking.

Drain the beans and put in a bowl. While still warm, stir in 1½ tablespoons of the oil, the spring onions, parsley and roasted pepper and yogurt sauce. Season to taste.

Thinly slice the avocados and sprinkle with the lime juice.

Arrange the lettuce and chicory on individual plates. Pile the beans in the middle and sprinkle with the diced pepper. Scatter the avocados and tomatoes round the edge.

Spoon some of the coriander and chilli cream over the avocados and tomatoes, and garnish with coriander or parsley.

QUINOA SALAD WITH PAPAYA, CUCUMBER AND ALMONDS

SERVES 2–3

Known as the food of the Incas, quinoa is packed with nutrients. It is particularly high in protein and carbohydrate, and is therefore a valuable source of energy for vegetarians. The pearly little seeds have a slightly bitter aftertaste which is counteracted here by the sweetness of the papaya and orange juice. You could use bulgar wheat instead.

⅓ cucumber (about 150 g/5 oz)
salt
2 tbsp light sesame oil
100 g/4 oz quinoa
250 ml/9 fl oz light stock
3 tbsp orange juice
1 small papaya
40 g/1½ oz almonds with skins, sliced lengthways
1½ tbsp snipped fresh chives
2 tsp tamari
2 tsp rice or white wine vinegar
freshly ground black pepper
2 handfuls trimmed rocket or watercress
1 Little Gem lettuce

Peel the cucumber and cut lengthways into 4. Remove the seeds. Cut the flesh crossways into thin segments. Put in a colander, sprinkle with salt and leave to drain for 30 minutes.

Heat 1 tablespoon of the sesame oil in a small saucepan. Add the quinoa and stir-fry over a medium heat for about 3 minutes until the quinoa smells toasty and starts to change colour. Add the stock and ¼ teaspoon of salt. Bring to the boil, then cover and simmer over a very low heat for 15 minutes. Remove from the heat, fluff with a fork and stir in 2 tablespoons of the orange juice. Leave to stand, covered, for 10 minutes. Transfer to a bowl and leave to cool.

Cut the papaya in half. Scoop out the seeds and reserve 2 teaspoonsful. Remove the skin and slice the flesh into small segments the same size as the cucumber. Sprinkle with the remaining orange juice.

Gently toss the quinoa with the papaya, cucumber, almonds and chives. Mix the tamari, rice vinegar, remaining sesame oil, and salt and pepper to taste. Pour over the quinoa and toss gently.

Arrange the salad leaves round the edge of a serving dish and pile the quinoa mixture on top. Garnish with the reserved papaya seeds.

QUINOA SALAD WITH BEAN SPROUTS, CUCUMBER, CHILLI AND PEANUTS

SERVES 4–6

This is delicious as it is, or you could top it with grilled prawns. You can make it a day or two ahead, but add the chives, bean sprouts and cucumber just before serving.

5 tbsp light sesame oil
200 g / 7 oz quinoa
1 tsp coriander seeds, crushed
seeds from 3 cardamom pods
1 tbsp chopped fresh thyme
600 ml / 1 pint vegetable stock
½ tsp salt
3 tbsp lemon juice
1 tbsp shoyu
75 g / 3 oz peanuts, roughly chopped
1 fresh green chilli, seeded and sliced
4 tbsp snipped fresh chives
200 g / 7 oz bean sprouts
100 g / 4 oz cucumber, quartered lengthways and sliced
salt and freshly ground black pepper
2 Little Gem lettuces

Heat 3 tablespoons of the oil in a saucepan. Add the quinoa, coriander seeds, cardamom and thyme, and stir-fry over a medium heat for about 3 minutes until the quinoa starts to colour. Add the stock and salt, bring to the boil. Cover and simmer over a low heat for 15 minutes.

Remove from the heat, fluff with a fork and stir in the lemon juice and shoyu. Cover again and leave to stand for 10 minutes. Transfer to a bowl.

Heat the remaining oil and stir-fry the peanuts and chilli until the peanuts are golden. Add to the quinoa with the oil. Carefully stir in the chives, bean sprouts and cucumber. Season to taste.

Arrange the lettuce round the edge of a serving dish and pile the quinoa mixture in the middle. Use the leaves to scoop up the grains.

BUTTERBEAN SALAD WITH SALAMI AND EGG

SERVES 2-3

You could substitute the salami with a can of drained tuna. Leave to stand for at least an hour before serving, or it can be made a day ahead.

175 g / 6 oz butterbeans, soaked overnight
salt
Basic Vinaigrette (page 187)
freshly ground black pepper
4–5 thin slices Italian salami, cut into narrow strips
1 large plum tomato, seeded and chopped
2 tbsp finely chopped red onion
10–12 pitted black olives, sliced
1 tbsp chopped fresh flat-leafed parsley
1 tbsp snipped fresh chives
handful of fresh basil leaves, torn
1 hard-boiled egg, finely chopped

Drain the beans and put in a saucepan with enough water to cover. Bring to the boil, then boil rapidly for 20 minutes. Continue to cook for a little longer until just tender, adding salt during the last 10 minutes of cooking. Drain and put in a serving bowl.

Pour the dressing over the beans while still warm and season to taste. Allow to cool.

Stir in the salami, tomato, onion, olives, parsley, chives and basil, and toss gently. Add more oil if necessary and check the seasoning. Sprinkle with the chopped egg.

TWO-GRAIN TABBOULEH

SERVES 2–3

Combining two different grains with lentils boosts the protein content as the different amino acids in each grain complement each other to make 'complete' protein. The salad improves with keeping and can be made a day ahead.

75 g/3 oz bulgar wheat
75 g/3 oz cooked brown rice (about 40g/1½ oz uncooked)
75 g/3 oz cooked Puy lentils (about 40g/1½ oz uncooked)
finely grated zest of 1 lemon
juice of ½ lemon
3 tbsp extra virgin olive oil
2 garlic cloves, finely chopped
salt and freshly ground black pepper
large handful of trimmed fresh coriander or flat-leafed parsley, chopped
large handful of fresh mint, chopped
2 spring onions, finely chopped
2 tomatoes, seeded and chopped
75 g/3 oz cucumber, seeded and finely chopped

Cover the bulgar wheat with boiling water and leave to soak for 1 hour. Rinse and drain thoroughly, then wrap in a clean tea-towel and squeeze out the remaining moisture. Mix with the rice, lentils and lemon zest.

In a large bowl, combine the remaining ingredients.

Carefully stir in the grains. Add more oil or lemon juice if necessary and check the seasoning. Leave to stand at room temperature for at least 1 hour to allow the flavours to develop.

PUY LENTILS WITH MINT AND SPROUTED BEANS

SERVES 2-3

Cooked lentils can be prepared ahead of time and will keep in the fridge for 3–4 days. Orange carrots and pale green avocado go beautifully with the lentils. As alternative accompaniments, you could use simple grated carrots dressed with a little orange juice and olive oil, or the Carrot, Orange and Ginger Salad (page 160), or the Guacamole (page 174).

175 g/6 oz Puy lentils
½ tsp dried chilli flakes
1 tsp cumin seeds
1 bay leaf
juice of 1 lemon
3 tbsp olive oil
3 tbsp chopped fresh mint
salt and freshly ground black pepper
150 g/5 oz mixed sprouted seeds and beans, such as alfafa,
chick-peas and mung beans
1 Little Gem lettuce
Carrot, Chicory and Pine Nut Salad (page 161)
Avocado and Smoked Tofu Dip (page 173)
or cottage cheese

Rinse the lentils and put in a saucepan with the chilli flakes, cumin seeds and bay leaf. Add 350 ml/12 fl oz water. Bring to the boil, then cover and simmer over a low heat for 25–30 minutes until just tender and the water has been absorbed. Drain if there is any excess water left.

Transfer the lentils to a bowl. Toss with the lemon juice,

olive oil, mint and seasoning while still warm. Allow to cool then mix in the sprouts.

Arrange the lettuce on individual plates with the lentils, carrot, chicory and pine nut salad, and the avocado and smoked tofu dip or cottage cheese on top.

LENTIL, CELERY AND EGG SALAD

SERVES 2–3

Puy lentils are a beautiful speckled purplish-brown colour with a satisfyingly earthy taste. They are rich in potassium, iron, zinc, selenium and B vitamins.

175 g/6 oz Puy lentils
1 small onion, finely chopped
juice and finely grated zest of ½ lemon
4 tbsp Mustard Vinaigrette (page 189)
salt and freshly ground black pepper
1 small leek
2 stalks celery, cut into thin diagonal slices
1 carrot, coarsely grated
2 tbsp chopped fresh lovage or flat-leafed parsley
4 rashers streaky bacon
15 g/½ oz butter
1 egg, beaten
3–4 handfuls cos lettuce, torn into bite-sized pieces

Rinse the lentils and put in a saucepan with the onion, lemon juice and zest, and 350 ml/12 fl oz water. Bring to the boil, then cover and simmer over a low heat for 25–30 minutes until just tender and the water has been absorbed. Drain the lentils if there is any excess water left.

While still warm toss with the vinaigrette and season to taste.

Cut the leek into 3 cm/1¼ inch pieces, then slice lengthways into thin shreds. Add to the lentils with the celery, carrot and half the lovage or parsley.

Grill the bacon until crisp, then slice into small pieces.

Heat the butter in a small non-stick pan until foaming. Add the egg, season to taste and cook until set. Remove from the pan and roll up. Slice into 1 cm/½ inch strips.

Arrange the lettuce in a shallow serving dish or on individual plates. Pile the lentil mixture in the middle. Scatter the egg strips and the bacon pieces over the lentils and garnish with the remaining lovage or parsley.

CHICK-PEA, SPINACH AND ROASTED PEPPER SALAD

SERVES 2–3

Delicious served with warmed pitta bread and yogurt, or Cucumber and Yogurt (page 167), or Coriander and Chilli Cream (page 200).

175 g/6 oz chick-peas, soaked overnight
6 tbsp olive oil
1 tbsp mustard seeds
350 g/12 oz young spinach, stalks removed
2 tbsp lemon juice
3 white cocktail onions, quartered lengthways
1 Roasted Pepper (page 178), diced
1 clove fresh or Roasted Garlic (page 183), finely chopped
1 fresh or Roasted Chilli (page 182), seeded and very finely chopped
2 tbsp chopped fresh coriander
salt and freshly ground black pepper
Coriander and Chilli Cream (page 200) or plain yogurt, to serve

Drain the chick-peas and put in a saucepan with plenty of water. Boil rapidly for 20 minutes, then continue to cook for a further 20–30 minutes until just tender. Add salt during the last 10 minutes of cooking.

Meanwhile, heat the oil in a pan with the mustard seeds until they start to pop. Add the spinach and stir-fry for 1–2 minutes until just wilted.

Remove from the heat, stir in the lemon juice, onions, pepper, garlic, chilli and coriander, and season to taste. Add the chick-peas and toss gently.

Arrange the spinach and chick-pea mixture on a plate and top with the coriander and chilli cream or yogurt.

CHICK-PEA SALAD WITH GREEN BEANS, ROASTED VEGETABLES, LEMON AND CUMIN

SERVES 2–3

This salad improves with standing. It will keep in the refrigerator for a few days, but make sure you allow it to come to room temperature before serving.

175 g/6 oz chick-peas, soaked overnight
6 tbsp olive oil
3 tbsp lemon juice
finely grated zest of 1 lemon
2 garlic cloves, finely chopped
1 tsp toasted cumin seeds, crushed
1 tsp dried thyme
salt and freshly ground black pepper
2 spring onions, chopped
75 g/3 oz cooked green beans, cut into 2 cm/¾ inch pieces
1 Roasted Courgette (page 180), cut into 2.5 cm/1 inch strips
1 Oven-Dried Aubergine (page 177), cut into 2.5 cm/1 inch strips
1 red Roasted Pepper (page 178), cut into matchstick strips
2 hard-boiled eggs, chopped
1 tbsp chopped fresh flat-leafed parsley or coriander
pitted black olives, to garnish

Drain the chick-peas, cover with water and boil briskly for 20 minutes. Continue to cook until just tender, then drain.

Combine the oil, lemon juice and zest, garlic, cumin, thyme, and salt and pepper in a large bowl. Add the chick-peas and toss while still warm. Leave to cool.

Stir in the spring onions, beans, courgette, aubergine and red pepper. Check the seasoning. Top with the eggs and sprinkle with the parsley or coriander, and olives.

COUSCOUS SALAD WITH CORIANDER AND MINT

SERVES 2–3

Serve this as it is, or add some chunks of leftover grilled meaty fish, diced grilled lamb or cooked prawns. Serve with Cucumber and Yogurt (page 167), or plain yogurt, and perhaps a spicy salsa. Harissa sauce is a fiery condiment popular in North African cooking. It is available in tubes or small cans.

150 g/5 oz couscous
5–6 tbsp olive oil
¼ tsp harissa
2 tbsp lemon juice
1 garlic clove, finely chopped
3 tbsp chopped fresh mint
3 tbsp chopped fresh coriander
salt and freshly ground black pepper
100 g/4 oz shredded green cabbage
50 g/2 oz blanched green beans, chopped
4 spring onions, green parts included, cut into 5 cm/2 inch pieces and shredded
½ yellow or green pepper, very thinly sliced
40 g/1½ oz toasted almonds with skins, halved lengthways

Put the couscous in a large bowl and pour over 250 ml/9 fl oz boiling water. Cover and leave to stand for about 10 minutes until the water is absorbed. Fluff the couscous with a fork.

Whisk together the oil, harissa, lemon juice, garlic, mint, coriander and seasoning. Pour over the salad and toss gently.

Stir in the remaining ingredients and toss carefully. Add more lemon juice, oil or seasoning if necessary.

BULGAR WHEAT SALAD WITH PINE NUTS, SPINACH, CARROT AND OLIVES

SERVES 2

A pretty light-textured salad of green and orange. Continue the green theme and serve it with a small vegetable salad and a dip. Any of the following would be fine: Kohlrabi Salad with Lemon and Lovage (page 155), Green Bean, Lemon and Sesame Salad (page 163), Cucumber and Yogurt (page 167), Avocado and Smoked Tofu Dip (page 173), Roasted Courgette, Lemon and Basil Salad (page 181).

150 g/5 oz bulgar wheat
2 handfuls young spinach, finely shredded
2 carrots, grated
10 pitted black olives
3 tbsp toasted pine nuts
2 tsp shoyu
1 tbsp light sesame oil
1 tbsp pine nut oil
freshly ground black pepper

Rinse the bulgar wheat in several changes of water until the water runs clear. Put in a bowl and cover with about 1 litre/1¾ pints of boiling water. Leave to soak for 2 hours. Drain off any excess water then put on a clean tea towel. Gather up the edges and twist the bulgar wheat into a ball, forcing out as much liquid as possible.

Put the dried bulgar wheat in a bowl with the spinach, carrots, olives and pine nuts. Add the shoyu, sesame and pine nut oils, and pepper. Toss well, then leave to stand at room temperature for 30 minutes before serving.

WHEATBERRY SALAD WITH SPRING VEGETABLES, LEMON, CORIANDER AND MINT

SERVES 2–3

Wheatberries are the whole grains from ears of wheat. Sold in healthfood shops, they are pleasantly chewy with a mellow flavour. You could use brown rice instead. This is just fine on its own but a few cubes of feta cheese will add sharpness and richness. The salad will keep for 2–3 days in the fridge but don't add the watercress until ready to serve.

175 g / 6 oz wheatberries
½ tsp salt
finely grated zest and juice of ½ lemon
2 tbsp chopped fresh mint
2 tbsp chopped fresh coriander
2 tsp shoyu
2 tbsp olive oil
freshly ground black pepper
3 dwarf courgettes
10 radishes
3 small carrots
2 handfuls trimmed watercress
50 g / 2 oz feta cheese, cubed (optional)

Rinse and drain the wheatberries. Put in a saucepan with the salt and enough water to cover by 2.5 cm/1 inch. Bring to the boil, then cover and simmer over a very low heat for 45–50 minutes until the berries are tender but still chewy.

Drain off any excess liquid and transfer to a bowl. Toss with the lemon juice, zest, mint, coriander, shoyu, olive oil and pepper while still warm. Allow to cool.

Slice the courgettes, radishes and carrots crossways into very thin circles. Add to the wheatberries.

Arrange the watercress round the edge of individual plates, with the wheatberries in the middle. Top with the cheese if using.

LIME AND PISTACHIO GREEN RICE SALAD

SERVES 3-4

This salad needs herbs with a lively flavour. I use sorrel, mint and rocket as those were the only ones still alive in my herb garden in early winter when I first made it. An unlikely combination but a happy one. You could eat this on its own, or with tuna or prawns, or the chicken as prepared in Chicken and Avocado Salad with Lime and Coriander (page 70).

600 g / 1¼ lb cooked white long-grain rice (250 g / 9 oz uncooked)
Lime and Pistachio Vinaigrette (page 191)
40 g / 1½ oz shelled pistachio nuts
4 spring onions, green parts included, finely chopped
50 g / 2 oz cooked peas
75 g / 3 oz cooked green beans, finely chopped
3 tbsp chopped fresh coriander
1 tbsp each chopped fresh mint, rocket and sorrel
salt and freshly ground black pepper
4 handfuls small spinach leaves, stalks removed

Put the rice in a large bowl. Pour the dressing over the rice and toss gently.

Cover the pistachio nuts with boiling water, leave for 5 minutes, then slip off the skins.

Mix the nuts, onions, peas, beans and herbs with the rice. Season to taste, then leave to stand for at least 30 minutes.

To serve, arrange the spinach leaves around the edge of a serving dish or individual plates. Pile the rice salad on top.

ORIENTAL RICE AND MIXED VEGETABLE SALAD

SERVES 2–3

This salad tastes really healthy – crunchy matchstick vegetables, chewy brown rice and a mellow shoyu dressing with a dash of sesame oil. Perfect for weightwatchers.

350–400 g/12–14 oz cooked brown rice
(about 150 g/5 oz uncooked)
1 carrot
1 courgette
1 tender celery stalk
½ small leek
handful of trimmed mangetout
¼ small red pepper
50 g/2 oz cucumber
1 tsp toasted sesame seeds
Oriental Vinaigrette (page 189)
few drops of toasted sesame oil
chopped spring onion tops, to garnish

Cut the carrot, courgette, celery and leek into matchstick strips. Plunge into boiling water for a few seconds with the mangetout. Drain under cold running water and pat dry thoroughly. Slice the mangetout diagonally into thirds.

Cut the red pepper and cucumber into matchstick strips.

Put the rice, vegetables and sesame seeds in a serving bowl and pour over enough dressing to coat. Sprinkle with the sesame oil and season to taste. Toss gently, adding more oil and seasoning if necessary. Sprinkle with the spring onion tops. Leave to stand at room temperature for 1 hour before serving.

PASTA, AUBERGINE AND ROCKET SALAD

SERVES 2–3

This can be prepared ahead of time, but don't add the rocket until just before serving.

150 g/5 oz pasta shapes, such as fusilli, penne or conchiglie
1 tbsp extra virgin olive oil
1 Oven-Dried Aubergine (page 177), cut into 2.5 cm/1 inch pieces
2 tbsp finely chopped onion
10 pitted black olives, halved
1 tbsp chopped fresh marjoram or thyme
¼–½ tsp dried chilli flakes
salt and freshly ground black pepper
4 handfuls trimmed rocket
Basic Vinaigrette (page 187)
Parmesan shavings

Cook the pasta in plenty of boiling salted water until 'al dente'. Drain, toss with the oil and leave to cool.

Put the pasta in a serving bowl and toss with the aubergine, onion, olives, marjoram, chilli flakes, and salt and pepper. Add the rocket and vinaigrette, and toss again. Sprinkle with Parmesan shavings and serve at once.

PASTA SALAD WITH CHEESE AND SALAMI

SERVES 2–3

Cheese and salami are undeniably high in fat, but here they are used in small quantities. They add rich flavours and contrast well with the blandness of the pasta.

150 g/5 oz penne or rigatoni
1 tbsp extra virgin olive oil
1 garlic clove, finely chopped
¼ tsp dried chilli flakes
freshly ground black pepper
2 tomatoes, seeded and cut into thin slivers
1 green pepper, seeded and cut into thin strips
2 spring onions, finely chopped
1 tbsp chopped fresh oregano or thyme
Basic Vinaigrette (page 187)
3 slices Italian salami, cut into thin strips
3 slices coppa or bresaola, cut into thin strips
75 g/3 oz taleggio or fontina cheese, diced
25 g/1 oz Parmesan cheese, shaved into wafers
10 pitted black olives
torn basil leaves, to garnish

Cook the pasta in plenty of boiling salted water until 'al dente'. Drain and toss with the oil, garlic, chilli flakes and pepper. Leave to cool.

Put the pasta in a large bowl with the tomatoes, green pepper, spring onions and oregano. Add the vinaigrette and toss gently.

Transfer the mixture to a shallow serving dish or individual plates. Arrange the meats and cheeses on top, then scatter over the olives and basil.

CONCHIGLIE, GREEN BEAN AND AVOCADO SALAD

SERVES 3–4

If you can't get hold conchiglie or gnocchi (shells), use any pasta shape which will trap chunky morsels in its crevices. Lumache (snails) or orecchiette (ears) would be fine.

200 g/7 oz conchiglie or gnocchi
1 large avocado or 1½ small ones
juice of 1 lime
1 garlic clove, finely chopped
150 ml/¼ pint plain yogurt
salt and freshly ground black pepper
75 g/3 oz cooked green beans, chopped
4 spring onions, chopped finely
1 red pepper, seeded and diced
4 tbsp chopped fresh flat-leafed parsley
6–8 slices Oven-Dried Aubergine (page 177), cut into 2 cm/¾ inch pieces
40 g/1½ oz toasted pine nuts
coarse sea salt

Cook the pasta in plenty of boiling salted water until 'al dente'. Drain thoroughly and cool.

Put the avocado flesh in a blender with the lime juice, garlic, yogurt, and salt and pepper. Purée briefly, so the mixture is fairly smooth but still with some avocado chunks.

Put the pasta in a bowl and toss with the avocado mixture, beans, spring onions, red pepper and 3 tablespoons of the parsley. Scatter the aubergine, pine nuts and remaining parsley on top. Sprinkle with a little coarse sea salt.

PASTA, COURGETTE AND ROSEMARY SALAD WITH SUN-DRIED TOMATOES

SERVES 2–3

Serve this with a simple green salad of mixed leaves and a small tomato salad for a delicious, light meal.

150 g/5 oz pasta shapes, such as conchiglie, lumache or gnocchi
1 tbsp extra virgin olive oil
2 tsp finely chopped fresh rosemary
finely grated zest of 1 lemon
2 small courgettes, grated
1 tbsp chopped fresh flat-leafed parsley
1½ tbsp toasted pine nuts
6 pieces oil-cured sun-dried tomatoes, chopped
Basic Vinaigrette (page 187)
salt and freshly ground black pepper

Cook the pasta in plenty of boiling salted water until 'al dente'. Drain and toss with the oil, rosemary and lemon zest. Leave to cool.

Transfer to a serving bowl and mix with the courgettes, parsley, pine nuts and sun-dried tomatoes. Toss with the vinaigrette and season to taste. Leave to stand for at least 1 hour before serving.

6

Small Salads, Dips, Salsas and Toppings

With their colour, moistness and tangy flavours, these dishes add the finishing touch to main meal salads. They also provide balance when a nutritional element is in short supply. For instance, small salads of leaves contribute vitamins and fibre to meat or fish salads; yogurt and cream-based dips and dressings, together with nuts, provide vegetable and leaf salads with protein.

There are no hard and fast rules as to what goes with what. Follow your tastebuds, with an eye for texture and colour, and use these as additional accompaniments.

KOHLRABI SALAD WITH LEMON AND LOVAGE

SERVES 3-4

Kohlrabi deserves to be used more often. It is a beautiful pale green with a crunchy texture and a slightly odd flavour, which seems to go very well with lemon and lovage. If you don't have any lovage, use flat-leafed parsley or celery leaves instead.

4 small kohlrabi
finely grated zest of 1½ lemons
3 tbsp chopped fresh lovage
1 tsp white wine vinegar
4 tbsp extra virgin olive oil
salt and freshly ground black pepper

Peel the kohlrabi and cut the flesh into 1 cm/½ inch dice. Mix with the lemon zest and lovage. Sprinkle with the vinegar and olive oil, and season to taste.

TOMATO AND BASIL SALAD

SERVES 2-3

Use small firm tomatoes with a good flavour.

350 g / 12 oz small tomatoes, quartered
pinch of sugar
salt and freshly ground black pepper
a few torn basil leaves
1 tbsp extra virgin olive oil

Put the tomatoes in a dish and sprinkle with sugar, and salt and pepper. Toss with the basil and olive oil.

OVEN-DRIED TOMATOES

SERVES 4

It's worth making these in quantity as they will keep in the fridge for several days. The slow baking really intensifies the flavour. Even tasteless tomatoes will benefit! Serve at room temperature with hot crusty bread, or add to a composed salad.

6 plum tomatoes, halved
3 tbsp olive oil
freshly ground black pepper
1 tsp muscovado sugar
pinch of fennel seeds (optional)

Pack the tomatoes in a single layer in a shallow ovenproof dish, into which they fit snugly. Sprinkle with the remaining ingredients and bake in a preheated oven at 150°C/300°F/gas 2 for about 2 hours until beginning to shrivel.

Remove from the dish with a slotted spoon.

ROASTED BEETROOT, RED PEPPER AND GARLIC SALAD WITH WALNUTS

SERVES 2-3

If you think you don't like beetroot — try this. Roasting it completely changes the flavour. The walnuts and the balsamic vinegar counteract the sweetness of the beetroot.

4–6 tbsp extra virgin olive oil
600 g / 1¼ lb uncooked beetroot, peeled and quartered
1 tsp dried chilli flakes
1 tbsp dried oregano
salt and freshly ground black pepper
3 large garlic cloves, unpeeled
1 red Roasted Pepper (page 178), diced
25 g / 1 oz shelled walnuts, chopped
1 tbsp walnut oil
1 tsp balsamic vinegar

Put the olive oil in a small roasting tin — there should be enough oil to cover the bottom of the tin. Heat the tin in an oven preheated to 200°C/400°F/gas 6. Add the beetroot, chilli flakes, oregano, and salt and pepper, stirring well. Roast for 40 minutes, turning occasionally.

Add the garlic and roast for another 40–45 minutes, basting with the juices, until the beetroot is tender and beginning to blacken at the edges.

Chop the beetroot pieces in half and transfer to a serving dish. Squeeze over the softened garlic and discard the skins. Add the red pepper and walnuts.

Sprinkle with the walnut oil and vinegar and serve warm or at room temperature.

MARINATED CARROT RIBBONS

SERVES 2

A colourful and tasty addition to a salad, providing valuable anti-oxidants: carotene (vitamin A), vitamins E and C.

3 carrots, cut into 5 cm / 2 inch lengths
½ tsp sugar
2 tsp cider or white wine vinegar
1 tbsp orange juice
2 tbsp extra virgin olive oil
salt and freshly ground black pepper

Using a swivel peeler, shave wide ribbons from opposite sides of the carrots, discarding the cores if they are woody.

Dissolve the sugar in the vinegar and orange juice. Whisk in the oil and seasonings, then add the carrots. Marinate for at least 2 hours or overnight.

CARROT, ORANGE AND GINGER SALAD

SERVES 3-4

Black kalonji (onion seeds) add a mysterious earthy flavour to this salad, and the colour contrasts beautifully with the carrots and oranges. Poppy seeds, or black cumin seeds would do instead but they have a different flavour.

2 small oranges
350 g / 12 oz carrots, grated
1.5 cm / ½ inch piece fresh ginger root
¼ tsp sugar
½ tsp kalonji (onion seeds)
salt and freshly ground black pepper
1 tbsp orange juice
2 tbsp olive oil

Peel the oranges making sure no white pith remains. Using a very sharp knife, slice thinly then cut into segments. Put in a bowl with the grated carrots.

Squeeze the ginger in a garlic press and mix the juice with the carrots and oranges.

Add the sugar, kalonji seeds and seasoning. Sprinkle with the orange juice and olive oil, and toss until well mixed.

CARROT, CHICORY AND PINE NUT SALAD

SERVES 2

Used in small quantities, pine nut oil is one of those luxuries which make a salad really special. If you don't have any, use extra virgin olive oil instead.

3 carrots
1 fat head of chicory, sliced crossways
2 tbsp toasted pine nuts
1 tbsp snipped fresh chives
1 tbsp chopped fresh lovage
½ tbsp white wine vinegar
1 tbsp orange juice
salt and freshly ground black pepper
2 tbsp light olive oil
2 tsp pine nut oil

Peel the carrots and cut in half crossways. Using a swivel peeler, shave away wide ribbons working from opposite sides. Put in a bowl with the chicory, pine nuts and herbs.

Whisk the remaining ingredients and toss with the salad.

MUSHROOM AND CORIANDER SALAD

SERVES 2–3

6 tbsp olive oil
450 g / 1 lb chestnut or button mushrooms, cut into segments
1 bay leaf
1 tsp coriander seeds, crushed
juice of 1 lemon
1 garlic clove, finely chopped
2 tbsp chopped flat-leafed parsley
salt and freshly ground black pepper

Heat the oil in a large pan. Add the mushrooms, bay leaf and coriander seeds. Stir-fry over a high heat for about 8 minutes until most of the liquid has evaporated, then add the lemon juice and garlic.

Reduce the heat and stir-fry for a few more minutes until the garlic is just golden.

Remove from the heat, transfer to a serving bowl and allow to cool. Stir in the parsley and salt and pepper.

GREEN BEAN, LEMON AND SESAME SALAD

SERVES 2

275 g / 10 oz green beans, trimmed
finely grated zest of ½ lemon
½ tsp toasted sesame seeds
salt and freshly ground black pepper
1 tbsp olive oil
few drops of dark sesame oil

Plunge the beans into plenty of boiling salted water for 3–4 minutes, until only just tender. They should be very crunchy. Drain and chop into 4 cm/1½ inch pieces.

Transfer to a bowl and stir in the remaining ingredients while still warm. Serve at room temperature.

CELERIAC REMOULADE

SERVES 4

Another classic worth including as it is the perfect addition to main meal salads based on fish or meat.

1 celeriac root
juice of 1 lemon
salt and freshly ground black pepper
150 ml / ¼ pint mayonnaise
2 tsp Dijon mustard
1 tbsp chopped fresh herbs, such as lovage, dill or chives, or a mixture

Peel the celeriac and grate coarsely using a food processor, or cut into matchstick strips. Immediately toss with the lemon juice, and salt and pepper. Cover and marinate for at least 30 minutes, then drain off any liquid.

Mix the mayonnaise with the mustard and herbs, and stir in the celeriac.

POTATO SALAD WITH YOGURT AND MINT

SERVES 3–4

large handful of trimmed fresh mint, finely chopped
1 Roasted Chilli (page 182), finely chopped
thumbnail-sized piece fresh ginger root, finely chopped
2 cloves Roasted Garlic (page 183), finely chopped
salt
150 ml / ¼ pint Greek yogurt
450 g / 1 lb small waxy new potatoes, unpeeled
1 tsp toasted sesame seeds
½ green pepper, seeded and diced
2 spring onions, chopped
dark sesame oil

Mix the mint, chilli, ginger, garlic and salt with the yogurt.

Boil the potatoes in their skins until just tender. Cut into even-sized pieces and toss with the yogurt mixture while still warm.

Stir in the sesame seeds, green pepper and spring onions. Sprinkle with a few drops of dark sesame oil.

MINTED RATATOUILLE

SERVES 3–4

The vegetables are cooked briefly so that they remain slightly crunchy and separate. This makes a good accompaniment to any of the lamb salads.

2 red onions
½ red pepper
½ yellow pepper
3 garlic cloves, finely chopped
1 small aubergine
2 small courgettes
2 firm plum tomatoes, peeled, seeded and finely chopped
about 5 tbsp olive oil
3 tbsp coarsely chopped fresh mint
coarse sea salt and freshly ground black pepper

Keeping each vegetable separate, cut them all into small even-sized dice.

Heat 2 tablespoons of the oil and gently fry the onion and peppers for 3 minutes until the onion is translucent. Add the garlic and fry for another 2 minutes. Remove from the pan and transfer to a colander to drain if necessary.

Add more oil to the pan, and stir-fry the aubergine until beginning to colour, adding a little water if it starts to stick. Remove from the pan and add to the colander. Repeat with the courgettes.

Return all the vegetables to the pan, and add the tomato. Stir in 2 tablespoons of the mint and cook for 1 minute more.

Season to taste and allow to cool to room temperature. Scatter with the remaining mint just before serving.

CUCUMBER AND YOGURT

SERVES 2

Cooling and refreshing to serve with hot spicy food. Drain the cucumber well, otherwise the salad will be watery.

¼ cucumber
salt
125 ml/4 fl oz Greek yogurt
1 garlic clove, finely chopped
1 tbsp finely chopped fresh mint
¼ tsp ground cumin
freshly ground pepper

Peel alternate strips of skin from the cucumber, slice lengthways into eighths, remove the seeds and chop the flesh finely. Put in a colander, sprinkle generously with salt and toss. Leave to drain for at least 30 minutes, then pat dry with paper towel.

Combine the remaining ingredients in a bowl, mixing well, then add the cucumber.

HUMMUS WITH LIME

SERVES 3–4

There are countless recipes for hummus, but it is so quickly made and has so many uses that it is worth including. The lime zest lifts the flavour and contrasts well with the earthy chick-peas. If you haven't got cooked chick-peas, use two 400 g/ 14 oz cans, drained and rinsed. You'll find they need less oil.

400 g/14 oz cooked chick-peas (about 200 g/7 oz uncooked)
finely grated zest and juice of 1–2 limes
2 garlic cloves, crushed
salt and freshly ground black pepper
150–300 ml/¼–½ pint olive oil

Put the chick-peas, lime zest and juice, garlic, and salt and pepper in a food processor. Purée until smooth, gradually pouring in the oil. Add a little water if necessary, and adjust the lime juice and seasoning to taste.

TOMATO AND CUCUMBER SALSA

SERVES 3–4

3 tomatoes, seeded and finely diced
200 g/7 oz cucumber, finely diced
1 garlic clove, finely chopped
2 spring onions, green parts included, finely chopped
1 small fresh chilli, seeded and finely chopped
finely grated zest and juice of ½ lime
¼ tsp finely grated orange zest
2 tbsp chopped fresh mint
1½ tbsp olive oil
pinch of salt

Combine all the ingredients in a small bowl. Cover and leave to stand at room temperature for 1–2 hours to let the flavours develop.

TOMATO AND AVOCADO SALSA

SERVES 2–3

4 tomatoes, seeded and diced
1 garlic clove, finely chopped
1 tbsp lime juice
1 avocado, diced
3 tbsp finely chopped red onion
1 small fresh chilli, finely chopped
2 tbsp chopped fresh coriander
2 tbsp olive oil
pinch of salt

Combine all the ingredients in a small bowl. Cover and leave to stand at room temperature for 1–2 hours before serving, to allow the flavours to mingle.

SMOKED SWEETCORN AND CHILLI SALSA

SERVES 3–4

Dry-frying gives the corn kernels a lovely smoky flavour. Use a heavy iron pan, rather than a non-stick one, and heat it thoroughly before adding the corn. The garlic clove needs to be only lightly roasted.

4 sweetcorn ears
½ tsp coarse sea salt
1–2 Roasted Chillies (page 182), chopped
1 clove Roasted Garlic (page 183), peeled and chopped
2 spring onions, green parts included, finely chopped
2 tomatoes, peeled, seeded and chopped
2 tbsp chopped fresh coriander
3 tbsp olive oil
2 tsp lime juice

Cut the kernels off the ears and mix with the salt. Transfer to a preheated heavy frying pan. Leave for a few seconds, then scrape them up and stir. Repeat this for 3–4 minutes, until the kernels are beginning to blacken and pop.

Place in a serving bowl and allow to cool. Stir in the remaining ingredients and serve at room temperature.

AUBERGINE, CHILLI AND SESAME DIP

SERVES 2–3

1 aubergine
1½ tbsp olive oil
3 tbsp yogurt
2 cloves Roasted Garlic (page 183)
1–2 Roasted Chillies (page 182)
1 tbsp toasted sesame seeds
¼ tsp salt
juice of 1 lemon
1 tsp toasted cumin seeds
chopped flat-leafed parsley, to garnish

Rub the aubergine with a little of the olive oil. Place on a baking sheet and roast in a preheated oven at 230°C/450°F/gas 8 for 25–30 minutes, until soft. Allow to cool, then remove the skin.

Put the aubergine in a food processor with the remaining oil and the other ingredients. Purée until smooth. Transfer to a bowl and garnish with parsley.

AVOCADO AND SMOKED TOFU DIP

SERVES 3–4

Smoked tofu adds a mysterious flavour which will keep your friends guessing. It also adds protein, calcium, B vitamins and vitamin E. This keeps better than most avocado dips, which tend to discolour quite quickly.

2 avocados, roughly chopped
175 g/6 oz smoked tofu
3 tbsp lemon juice
2 tbsp chopped fresh coriander or flat-leafed parsley
pinch of cayenne
salt and freshly ground black pepper

Put the avocado in a food processor with the remaining ingredients. Purée until smooth.

GUACAMOLE

SERVES 3–4

I like guacamole to have some texture, so I purée it very briefly.
Use very ripe avocados, and don't leave guacamole hanging
around – it will turn an unappetising shade of grey.

2–3 avocados
juice of 2 limes
1 large tomato, peeled, seeded and chopped
2 fresh chillies, seeded and chopped
2 tbsp finely chopped onion
1 tbsp chopped fresh coriander or flat-leafed parsley
salt

Put everything in a blender and purée until smooth but still
with some texture.

CARAMELISED ONION RINGS

Grilled until slightly blackened and crisp, onion rings add colour and succulent flavour to any main meal salad.

Using a very sharp knife, cut a peeled onion horizontally into 5 mm/¼ inch thick slices. Keep the rings in place by inserting 2 or 3 wooden cocktail sticks from the outside to the centre.

Brush each side with oil and place under a preheated very hot grill or over hot coals. Grill for 5–7 minutes each side until beginning to blacken round the edges.

TOMATO-FLAVOURED RED ONION CONFIT

SERVES 3–4

This is based on a tomato sauce recipe by Marcella Hazan. In her recipe she discards the onions, but I think they are almost the best bit. They take on a wonderfully rich tomato flavour and are also delicious in salads or served on slices of grilled polenta. Eat them warm or at room temperature. They will keep for about a week in a covered container in the fridge.

3 × 400 g / 14 oz cans chopped tomatoes
3 red onions, halved lengthways
175 g / 6 oz butter
salt

Put everything in a saucepan over a medium-low heat and stir until the butter has melted. Simmer over a low heat for about 50 minutes. Leave to cool.

Fish out the onions, scraping off any excess sauce. Thinly slice lengthways, and enjoy.

OVEN-DRIED
AUBERGINES

Oven-dried aubergines have a deeply satisfying sweetish, meaty flavour, which is totally addictive. Roasted until slightly crisp and blackened, I find them as tempting and 'more-ish' as a plate of chips. But they're better for you. Aubergines contain some protein, and useful amounts of potassium, calcium, magnesium, iron, vitamin E and folate – vital for cell formation and particularly needed during pregnancy.

Use firm, plump aubergines and slice them in half lengthways. Turn them cut side down and slice lengthways again into 5mm/¼ inch strips. Lightly brush the strips on both sides with olive oil. Arrange in a single layer in a large preheated roasting tin, or two smaller tins. Make sure there is plenty of space between the strips, otherwise they will steam in their own moisture and not become crisp.

Roast in a preheated oven at 240°C/475°F/gas 9, turning from time to time, for 15–20 minutes, until golden and slightly blackened at the edges. Add a little more oil if they begin to stick.

They will keep for 3–4 days in the fridge and make a great addition to a main meal salad.

ROASTED PEPPERS

Intensely flavoured and packed with vitamins and minerals, roasted peppers are a vital ingredient in main meal salads. It's worth keeping a few in a screw-top jar in the fridge. They'll last for 3 or 4 days.

Red peppers contain twenty times more carotene (vitamin A) than yellow ones, so use these unless you particularly want the yellow ones for colour. Green peppers are not so fleshy and are better eaten raw.

Place the whole peppers in a roasting tin and roast in a preheated oven at 230°C/450°F/gas 8 for 15–20 minutes until the skin blisters and blackens. Turn them frequently so the skin chars evenly. Alternatively, grill them on a rack over hot coals or under a preheated very hot grill, or place them directly over a gas flame, turning until evenly charred.

Allow to cool, then peel away the skin and remove the tops and seeds, saving the syrupy juices to mix with the dressing. Some cooks put the peppers in a sealed plastic bag for a few minutes to loosen the skin, but I have found this necessary only when you grill them over a gas flame. Don't peel the peppers under a running tap or you will lose the delicious smoky flavour.

If part of another dish, use as directed in the recipe. Otherwise, make a small roasted pepper salad.

ROASTED PEPPER SALAD

SERVES 2-3

2 large red or yellow Roasted Peppers, peeled and seeded
2 garlic cloves, finely chopped
dried red chilli flakes, to taste (optional)
salt and freshly ground black pepper
extra virgin olive oil
balsamic vinegar or lemon juice
chopped fresh flat-leafed parsley, coriander or basil leaves
pitted black olives, sliced

Dice or cut the peppers' flesh into thin strips and mix with the juices. Add the garlic and chilli, if using. Season to taste and toss with oil and a dash of vinegar or lemon juice. Sprinkle with herbs and a few pitted and sliced black olives.

ROASTED COURGETTES

Together with peppers and aubergines, roasted courgettes make a richly flavoured addition to a Mediterranean-style salad. Prepared this way, they retain maximum nutrients. They contain useful amounts of potassium, magnesium, calcium, iron, carotene (vitamin A) and vitamin C.

Choose medium-sized, firm courgettes. Trim the ends and slice them lengthways into four quadrants. Lightly brush with oil and spread out, cut side down, in a single layer in a large preheated roasting tin. It's important that the tin and the oven are very hot and the courgettes are well spaced out, otherwise they tend to steam in their own moisture and not brown up nicely. Roast in a preheated oven at 230°C/450°F/gas 8, turning occasionally, for 20–30 minutes until golden.

If part of another dish, use as directed in the recipe. Otherwise make a small roasted courgette, lemon and basil salad.

ROASTED COURGETTE, LEMON AND BASIL SALAD

SERVES 3–4

6 roasted courgettes
1 tsp grated lemon zest
2 tbsp torn basil leaves
salt and freshly ground black pepper
2 tbsp extra virgin olive oil
squeeze of lemon juice

Cut the roasted courgette slices into 4cm/1½ inch pieces. Mix with the lemon zest, basil leaves and seasoning. Sprinkle with the olive oil and lemon juice, then leave to stand at room temperature for an hour to let the flavours develop.

ROASTED CHILLIES

Although we don't eat them in large quantities, chillies make a healthy addition to salads. Weight for weight, a fresh red chilli contains six times more carotene (vitamin A) than a tomato and thirteen times more vitamin C. They are rich in potassium, which we need for healthy nerve and muscle function, and they contain useful amounts of calcium.

In most cases red and green chillies are interchangeable. Red chillies are riper than green and have a slightly sweeter flavour.

Roasted chillies are an entirely different taste sensation to the sharp fieriness of fresh ones. Roasting mellows the heat and brings out the full earthy flavour. The skin peels off easily and the flesh can be cut into strips to use in a salsa or as a zesty garnish, or it can be puréed and added to dips and dressings.

Roast only firm fleshy specimens. Place on a baking sheet in a preheated oven at 230°C/450°F/gas 8 and roast for 10–15 minutes, turning occasionally, until the skin blisters and blackens. Alternatively, hold them directly over a gas flame. Do not over-roast or the flesh will fall apart.

Allow to cool, then peel off the skins and remove the seeds. Don't do this under a running tap or you will wash away the delicious smoky flavour. Roast several chillies at a time and store them in an airtight container in the fridge. They will keep for two or three days.

ROASTED GARLIC

Eaten regularly, garlic is positively beneficial to good health. It helps lower the blood cholesterol associated with coronary heart disease, and it is rich in vitamin C, iron and potassium. Garlic is also one of the best sources of germanium – a mineral trace element believed to help boost the immune system; and of selenium, another trace element, with anti-oxidant properties similar to those of vitamin E.

Roasted garlic cloves produce a heavenly, gooey purée with a mellow flavour quite unlike that of raw or fried garlic. Smear it on crusty bread, whisk it into dips and dressings, or add it to cooked vegetable salads. Roast whole heads at a time and store them in an airtight container in the fridge. They will keep for a week or so. Use only firm plump heads, and avoid those which have started to sprout shoots.

Whole roasted garlic heads can also be used as a vegetable in their own right. Slice the heads in half horizontally, and roast cut side up. Otherwise remove as much of the papery skin as possible, still keeping the heads intact and roast whole.

Place in a shallow ovenproof dish and pour over about 5 tablespoons of olive oil. Roast in a preheated oven at 180°C/350°F/gas 4 for about 40 minutes, basting occasionally with the juices, until the cloves feel soft.

Quicker still, roast individual unpeeled cloves under a hot grill for about 10 minutes.

GARLIC CROUTONS

MAKES 100 G/4 OZ, ENOUGH FOR 2–3 SALADS

Use ciabatta, French bread, day-old crusty white loaf or good quality wholemeal bread. Don't remove the crusts. Croutons will keep for a few days in an airtight container.

4 tbsp olive oil
2 garlic cloves, thinly sliced
100 g/4 oz 1 cm/½ inch bread cubes

Heat the oil in a large frying pan. Gently fry the garlic for about 2 minutes until just golden. Remove with a slotted spoon.

Add the bread and fry over a medium heat for about 5 minutes until golden and crisp on all sides.

Remove from the pan and drain on paper towel.

Variations:

For Herbed Croutons, add 2 teaspoons mixed dried herbs to the pan with the bread.

For Chilli Croutons, add 1–2 seeded dried red chillies to the pan with, or instead of, the garlic. Remove with a slotted spoon before adding the bread.

GRILLED POLENTA

You can only cook polenta in generous quantities, but leftovers quickly disappear. Should you be left with an unused portion, cut it into squares or diamonds, put in a sealed plastic bag and store in the fridge or freezer. The cooled polenta can be cut into shapes, brushed with oil and grilled until crisp. Or cut it into small cubes, fry and use like croutons.

250 g/9 oz polenta
1 tsp salt
1 litre/1¾ pints water
olive oil

Put the polenta, salt and water in a large saucepan. Slowly bring to the boil, stirring constantly to remove any lumps. Cook for 20 minutes, continuing to stir, until the mixture comes away from the side of the pan.

Pour into a greased 30.5 × 23 cm/12 × 9 inch Swiss roll tin. Allow to cool and become firm, then turn out on to a board and cut into squares, oblongs or diamonds.

When ready to use, brush with oil and toast under a hot grill or in the oven, until crisp and lightly browned on both sides.

Variation:

For Polenta Croutons, cut the cooled polenta into small cubes and fry in hot oil until crisp. Drain on paper towel.

7

Dressings and Sauces

Dressings and sauces stimulate the taste buds and provide nutritional balance in cases where a nutrient is in short supply. For instance, yogurt and cream dressings provide vegetable and leaf salads with protein.

Although the recipes often specify a particular dressing, you can mix and match as you please.

When making vinaigrette dressings, bear in mind that the intensity of the vinegar may vary and adjust the amount according to taste. I am not a great lover of sharp dressings so I usually base mine on one part vinegar to six parts oil.

BASIC VINAIGRETTE

MAKES ABOUT 125 ML / 4 FL OZ

1½ tbsp white wine vinegar
½ tsp Dijon mustard
¼ tsp salt
freshly ground black pepper
6 tbsp extra virgin olive oil

Mix the vinegar with the mustard, salt and pepper, then whisk in the oil.

BALSAMIC VINAIGRETTE

MAKES ABOUT 125 ML / 4 FL OZ

Balsamic vinegar adds an intense richness to salads and consequently goes well with robust ingredients which can stand up to its penetrating aroma. Roasted vegetables, mushrooms, spinach and red cabbage are ideal partners. Use it sparingly and always in addition to regular wine vinegar.

1 tbsp red wine vinegar
½ tbsp balsamic vinegar
¼ tsp salt
freshly ground black pepper
6 tbsp extra virgin olive oil

Mix the vinegars with the seasonings, then whisk in the oil.

WALNUT VINAIGRETTE

MAKES ABOUT 125 ML / 4 FL OZ

½ tbsp white wine vinegar
½ tbsp balsamic vinegar
½ tsp Dijon mustard
¼ tsp salt
freshly ground black pepper
3 tbsp light olive oil or grapeseed oil
3 tbsp walnut oil

Combine the vinegar, mustard and seasonings, then whisk in the oils.

HAZELNUT VINAIGRETTE

MAKES ABOUT 125 ML / 4 FL OZ

1½ tbsp white wine vinegar
½ tsp Dijon mustard
¼ tsp salt
freshly ground black pepper
3 tbsp light olive oil or grapeseed oil
3 tbsp hazelnut oil

Combine the vinegar, mustard and seasonings, then whisk in the oils.

ORIENTAL VINAIGRETTE

MAKES ABOUT 125 ML / 4 FL OZ

Shoyu, or Japanese soy sauce, has a mellow salty flavour, so add extra salt sparingly or even leave it out. The dressing is delicious on seafood, sea vegetables, chicken, mushrooms and noodles. It also adds zest to light grains, such as quinoa and bulgar wheat.

2 tsp rice or cider vinegar
2 tsp shoyu
$\frac{1}{4}$ tsp sugar
salt and freshly ground black pepper
6 tbsp extra virgin olive oil
$\frac{1}{2}$ tsp toasted sesame oil

Mix together the vinegar, shoyu, sugar, and salt and pepper, then whisk in the oils.

MUSTARD VINAIGRETTE

MAKES 175 ML / 6 FL OZ

This is a strong zesty dressing, ideal for meat-based salads.

3 tbsp Dijon mustard
$3\frac{1}{2}$ tbsp wine vinegar
salt and freshly ground black pepper
125 ml / 4 fl oz extra virgin olive oil

Put the mustard, vinegar and seasonings in a blender and whizz until well blended. Gradually pour in the oil with the motor running and whizz until very thick.

CUMIN AND LIME VINAIGRETTE

MAKES ABOUT 150 ML/5 FL OZ

A tangy dressing ideal for fish and seafood salads. It also goes well with beans and chick-peas.

juice of 1 lime
1 tsp balsamic vinegar
1 garlic clove, finely chopped
1 tsp ground cumin
salt and freshly ground black pepper
6 tbsp extra virgin olive oil

Mix together the lime juice, vinegar, garlic, cumin, and salt and pepper, then whisk in the oil.

LIME AND PISTACHIO VINAIGRETTE

MAKES ABOUT 125 ML/4 FL OZ

A rich luxuriant dressing which adds depth to rice salads, or any leaf salad.

finely grated zest and juice of 1 lime
1 tbsp white wine vinegar
¼ tsp salt
freshly ground black pepper
4 tbsp light olive oil
4 tbsp pistachio oil

Mix together the lime zest and juice, vinegar and seasonings, then whisk in the oils.

PUMPKIN SEED VINAIGRETTE

MAKES ABOUT 125 ML/4 FL OZ

A toasty-flavoured dressing which echoes the pumpkin seeds in salads. It goes well with green beans, cabbage and kohlrabi, or freshly grated root vegetables.

1 tbsp wine vinegar
½ tsp Dijon mustard
¼ tsp salt
freshly ground black pepper
3 tbsp light olive oil
3 tbsp pumpkin seed oil

Mix together the vinegar, mustard and seasonings, then whisk in the oils.

ORANGE VINAIGRETTE

MAKES 175 ML/6 FL OZ

5 tbsp orange juice
1 tbsp balsamic vinegar
1 tsp Dijon mustard
salt and freshly ground black pepper
6 tbsp extra virgin olive oil

Combine the orange juice, vinegar, mustard and seasonings, then whisk in the oil.

ORANGE AND GINGER VINAIGRETTE

MAKES 125 ML / 4 FL OZ

This is delicious on poultry salads, particularly duck. It also goes well with grated carrot.

2 tbsp orange juice
2 tsp rice or cider vinegar
salt and freshly ground black pepper
2 cm / ¼ inch piece fresh ginger root, peeled
6 tbsp extra virgin olive oil

Mix the orange juice, vinegar and seasonings. Put the ginger in a garlic press and squeeze the juices into the dressing. Whisk in the oil.

JAPANESE HORSERADISH VINAIGRETTE

MAKES 125 ML/4 FL OZ

Wasabi is the ground root of a type of horseradish, available from good health food shops. Mixed to a paste with water, it makes a pungent condiment with a bright fresh flavour which cuts the richness of smoked salmon and prawns.

1 tbsp shoyu
½ tbsp rice vinegar
½ tsp sugar
2 tsp wasabi paste
5 tbsp light sesame oil

Combine the shoyu, vinegar, sugar and wasabi paste, then whisk in the sesame oil.

ROASTED PEPPER DRESSING

MAKES 150 ML/5 FL OZ

A colourful dressing ideal for bland cooked root vegetables.

1 red Roasted Pepper (page 178), chopped
2 cloves Roasted Garlic (page 183), chopped
1 tbsp white wine vinegar
1 tsp powdered oregano
salt and freshly ground black pepper
125 ml/4 fl oz extra virgin olive oil

Put all the ingredients in a blender and whizz for 2–3 minutes until thick and very smooth.

WALNUT CITRUS DRESSING

MAKES 100 ML/3½ FL OZ

1 tbsp orange juice
1 tbsp lime juice
½ tsp Dijon mustard
salt and freshly ground black pepper
3 tbsp light olive oil
3 tbsp walnut oil

Combine the fruit juices with the mustard and seasonings, then whisk in the oils.

GINGER CHILLI DRESSING

MAKES 125 ML / 4 FL OZ

Use this on any oriental-style salad where you want a burst of flavour.

2.5 cm / 1 inch piece fresh ginger root
1 Roasted Chilli (page 182), seeded and very finely chopped
finely grated zest of 1 lime
1 tbsp lime juice
salt and freshly ground black pepper
4 tbsp light sesame oil

Put the ginger in a garlic press and squeeze the juice into a small bowl. Add the chilli, lime zest and juice, and salt and pepper, mixing well. Whisk in the sesame oil.

WALNUT AND GREEN PEPPERCORN DRESSING

MAKES 125 ML / 4 FL OZ

An aromatic dressing ideal for poultry or meat-based salads.

2 tbsp lemon juice
2 tsp green peppercorns, crushed
salt
3 tbsp light olive oil
3 tbsp walnut oil

Mix the lemon juice with the peppercorns and salt, then whisk in the oils.

HAZELNUT AND LIME DRESSING

MAKES 125 ML / 4 FL OZ

The warm sweetness of hazelnuts and the sharpness of lime are delicious on any green leaf salad, particularly those containing avocado, asparagus or papaya.

2 tbsp lime juice
finely grated zest of 1 lime
salt and freshly ground black pepper
4 tbsp hazelnut oil
2 tbsp grapeseed or light olive oil

Mix together the lime juice, zest and seasoning, then whisk in the oils.

LIME AND CORIANDER DRESSING

MAKES ABOUT 100 ML / 3½ FL OZ

A Mexican-style dressing with a hint of fire. It's great on avocados or cooked black beans.

1 garlic clove, finely chopped
½ tsp grated lime zest
juice of ½ lime
1 tbsp very finely chopped fresh coriander
⅛ tsp dried chilli flakes
salt and freshly ground black pepper
pinch of sugar
4 tbsp extra virgin olive oil

Mix together the garlic, lime zest and juice, coriander, chilli flakes, salt and pepper, and sugar. Whisk in the oil.

LEMON YOGURT DRESSING

MAKES ABOUT 175 ML / 6 FL OZ

150 ml / ¼ pint plain yogurt
1 tbsp white wine vinegar
1 tsp lemon juice
pinch of finely grated lemon zest
salt and coarsely ground black pepper

Combine the yogurt, vinegar, lemon juice and zest, and season to taste.

HORSERADISH AND LEMON DRESSING

MAKES ABOUT 200 ML/7 FL OZ

150 ml/¼ pint plain yogurt
2 tbsp mayonnaise
finely grated zest of 1 lemon
1 tbsp freshly grated horseradish
salt and freshly ground black pepper

Combine the yogurt and mayonnaise. Stir in the lemon zest and horseradish, and season to taste.

CREAMY HERB DRESSING

MAKES 150 ML/5 FL OZ

1 tbsp wine vinegar
1 shallot, finely chopped
2 tsp chopped mixed fresh herbs
salt and freshly ground black pepper
2 tbsp extra virgin olive oil
5 tbsp low-fat yogurt
1 tbsp soured cream

Combine the vinegar, shallot, herbs, and salt and pepper in a small bowl. Whisk in the oil until thickened, then whisk in the yogurt and soured cream.

CORIANDER AND CHILLI CREAM

MAKES ABOUT 300 ML/½ PINT

Don't be tempted to purée the greenery with the yogurt and cream unless you want a very runny sauce. Chopping the coriander before puréeing may seem like a waste of time, but if you don't do it you'll end up with an unpleasantly stringy mixture. This is probably my favourite dressing. Use it on chicken, prawns, avocados, pulses, or just as a dip.

100 g/4 oz fresh coriander, trimmed and chopped
2 spring onions, chopped
1 garlic clove, crushed
½ Roasted Chilli (page 182), chopped
finely grated zest of 1 lime
2 tbsp lime juice
1 tsp toasted cumin seeds
salt and freshly ground black pepper
125 ml/4 fl oz Greek yogurt
75 ml/3 fl oz double cream

Put all the ingredients except the yogurt and cream in a food processor. Purée for 3 minutes, scraping the sides of the container frequently. Pour into a bowl and stir in the yogurt and cream.

ROASTED PEPPER AND YOGURT SAUCE

MAKES ABOUT 300 ML / ½ PINT

Wholemilk organic yogurt is absolutely delicious. It's more like clotted cream or creamy custard, and has a yellow crust on top. However, thick Greek yogurt is a reasonable alternative. Sun-dried tomato paste is available from delicatessens and good supermarkets. Make your own by whizzing up sun-dried tomatoes and olive oil in a blender. This is lemony, fiery and fresh-tasting – great on root vegetables.

2 Roasted Peppers (page 178), roughly chopped
1 Roasted Chilli (page 182), roughly chopped
6 tbsp wholemilk organic yogurt
3 tbsp sun-dried tomato paste
2 tbsp extra virgin olive oil
1 tsp toasted coriander seeds, crushed
1.5 cm / ½ inch piece fresh ginger root, finely chopped
1 tsp finely grated lemon zest
salt and freshly ground black pepper

Put all the ingredients in a blender and purée until smooth. This will keep for a week in the fridge.

INDONESIAN PEANUT DRESSING

MAKES 300 ML/½ PINT

Oriental ingredients can be bought from ethnic stores as well as from some of the larger supermarkets. Coconut milk can be bought in tins or as a powder and made up with warm water.

1 tbsp coconut or groundnut oil
½ small onion, finely chopped
2–3 fresh green chillies, seeded and chopped
2 garlic cloves, finely chopped
2 thin slices fresh ginger root
½ tsp blachan (shrimp paste)
100 g/4 oz roasted peanuts or crunchy peanut butter
1 tsp muscovado sugar
1 tsp ketjap manis (Indonesian soy sauce)
1 tbsp lemon juice or vinegar
½ tsp salt
225 ml/8 fl oz thick coconut milk

Heat the oil in a small pan. Gently fry the onion, chillies, garlic and ginger over a medium heat for 2–3 minutes. Stir in the blachan and stir-fry for another minute.

Transfer the mixture to a blender and grind to a paste. Add the peanuts and grind roughly. Add the sugar, ketjap manis, lemon juice, salt and coconut milk and blend again. The mixture should still have some texture.

Put the mixture in a saucepan, bring to the boil and simmer until thickened. Add some water if necessary. The mixture should be of pouring consistency.

8
Glossary of Salad Ingredients

The joy of main meal salads is that there isn't a time of year when ingredients are in short supply. If something is out of season a substitute can easily be found. Some of the ingredients I have used may be unfamiliar. In most cases I have suggested an alternative, but it is worth trying to find the more obscure items so that you can experience new tastes, and expand your salad-making repertoire.

The larger supermarkets now have such an enormous range that locating ingredients should not be a problem. Street markets, ethnic shops, healthfood shops and specialist mail order food companies are also good sources.

STOCKING UP

The following may sound a lot, but you don't have to buy the items all at once and many of them you will already have. However, many of them are used time and time again in salad-making, and are well worth the investment.

Storecupboard checklist

Oils, vinegars and seasonings

light olive oil
good quality extra virgin
   olive oil
walnut oil
hazelnut oil
pistachio, pine nut or
   pumpkin seed oil
   (or all three)
light sesame oil
toasted sesame oil
sunflower or safflower oil
   (preferably unrefined)

groundnut (peanut) oil
   (preferably unrefined)
wine vinegar
balsamic vinegar
sherry vinegar
rice vinegar
shoyu or tamari (Japanese
   soy sauce)
wasabi (Japanese horseradish)
harissa sauce
Dijon mustard

Herbs and spices

cumin seeds
coriander seeds
fennel seeds
kalonji (onion seeds)
dried oregano or thyme
bay leaves

dried chilli flakes
dried whole chillies
coarse sea salt
black peppercorns
green peppercorns

Nuts and seeds

pine nuts
walnut halves
peanuts
cashew nuts
hazel nuts
Brazil nuts

pistachio nuts
almonds
pumpkin seeds
sunflower seeds
sesame seeds

Noodles, grains and pulses

dried pasta shapes (Italian
    brands are best)
rice noodles
thin egg noodles
basmati rice
bulgar wheat
couscous
quinoa

polenta
black turtle beans
kidney beans
haricot beans
flageolet beans
chick-peas
Puy lentils

Cans and bottles

canned chopped tomatoes
tomato purée
canned palm hearts
canned tuna
anchovy fillets

canned sardines
bottled artichokes
oil-cured sun-dried tomatoes
olives
capers

Fridge checklist

peppers, courgettes,
    aubergines, garlic,
    chillies (fresh and
    roasted)
salad leaves
baby spinach
fresh herbs
lemons, limes, oranges
fresh ginger root
cooked potatoes
cooked green beans
cooked rice
cooked pulses, chick-peas,
    lentils

sprouted beans and seeds
ham
salami
cooked poultry
cooked meats
smoked fish
eggs
plain yogurt
Parmesan, goat's cheese,
    cottage cheese,
    mozzarella, feta
soured cream
whipping cream

Freezer checklist

ciabatta bread   prawns
pitta bread   chicken breasts
broad beans   barbary duck breasts
sweetcorn kernels

SALAD LEAVES

Supermarkets today stock a wonderful abundance of previously hard-to-find salad leaves. The leaves from young raw vegetables, such as spinach, chard and kale, can also be used in salads. Experiment with different types of leaves, and if possible try growing some of the more unusual ones yourself – even in a grow-bag or window box. Rocket and sorrel grow like weeds so there really is no need to buy these in expensive little packets from supermarkets.

There are also some very good mail order catalogues from which you can order seeds for exotic salad leaves, such as mizuna (Japanese salad), Chinese and Indian mustard greens and Thai salad leaves.

Many wild and garden plants have edible leaves, but don't use anything unless you're absolutely sure of its identity, and don't use leaves picked from the road-side verges.

Storing and washing salad leaves

Salad leaves are mostly water but they are a good source of dietary fibre, carotene (which converts to vitamin A), vitamin C and folate (one of the B vitamins). They also contain minerals such as potassium, calcium and iron. However, nutrient levels are quickly reduced if the leaves are not stored, washed and prepared correctly.

Always buy fresh, bright-looking leaves and discard any broken or wilted ones. Handle with care to avoid bruising. Wrap in paper or store in a plastic bag in the salad drawer of the fridge; they should keep for a few days.

When ready to use, wash the leaves under cold running water. Do not soak them or water-soluble vitamins will leach out. Dry in a salad spinner and remove as much water as possible, otherwise the dressing will be diluted. Pat dry with paper towel.

Tear the leaves rather than cutting them, to avoid bruising at the edges, but firm varieties such as Webbs or Chinese leaves can be shredded with a knife.

Dressing salads

Add the dressing at the very last minute, using just enough to barely coat the leaves. Avoid at all costs a salad swimming in oil. I agree with the Spanish saying which states that for a perfect salad dressing a miser should administer the vinegar, a spend-thrift the oil, and a madman should mix it.

Beet greens

Dark green leaves with red stems. Use only the youngest tenderest leaves and discard the stems. They taste of both beetroot and spinach.

Chicory

Long, yellow and white or red and white, tightly curled heads with slightly bitter spears and a crisp texture.

Chinese leaves

Elongated heads of white, densely packed leaves and crunchy stalks with a peppery flavour.

Escarole (batavia)

A broad-leafed type of frisee (curly endive), green on the outside with a pale yellow heart and a slightly bitter flavour.

Frisee (curly endive)

Large heads of thin crinkly leaves, dark green on the outside and pale yellow in the centre. They have a bitter, pungent flavour.

Lamb's lettuce (corn salad, mache)

This is not a true lettuce but a weed grown widely in France and Italy. The small tender dark green leaves bruise easily. They have a chewy texture, and a beautiful nutty sweetish flavour. Useful in winter, expensive to buy, but easy to grow.

Lettuce

There are four main types of lettuce: iceberg, cos, butterhead varieties and loose-leafed varieties. Iceberg (Webbs Wonder) is 90 per cent water, relatively tasteless and best used with a powerful dressing. Use it when a crisp texture is more important than flavour. Cos (or romaine) has long succulent pungent dark green leaves with a sweeter pale yellow heart. Little Gem lettuce is a smaller version of cos. Butterhead varieties have softly folded pale yellow sweet leaves. Loose-leafed lettuces have attractive large brownish-red and green leaves which are good for lining serving bowls. Varieties include Red Oak (feuille de chêne), Lollo Rosso and Lollo Biondo (both of more use for appearance than flavour), Salad Bowl and Four Seasons.

Mustard greens (Indian, Japanese and Chinese)

Delicious tender green leaves with a mustardy tang, which go well with milder-flavoured leaves. Grow your own or buy them from ethnic shops.

Radicchio

A round, deep red variety of chicory with a firm texture and a pleasant, slightly bitter flavour.

Rocket

A superb salad green with delicious rich peppery-flavoured leaves. Resistant to most plant pests and diseases, it can be grown almost all the year round.

Sorrel

A sharp lemon-flavoured leaf which resembles young spinach. Use only the smallest freshest leaves. It has a high oxalic acid content and should be eaten only in small quantities. Mix it with sweeter tasting leaves. Easy to grow and expensive to buy.

Spinach

Young crisp dark green leaves are excellent used raw in salads. Remove the stalks and tear the leaves into bite-sized pieces. Use within a day or two of buying it as the leaves quickly become slimy. Spinach is very rich in vitamins A and C, but it also contains oxalic acid and should not be eaten in Popeye-like quantities.

Watercress

The dark glossy leaves have a distinctive peppery flavour. Use within a day or two of purchase as the leaves quickly turn yellow. Watercress is rich in carotene (vitamin A), vitamin C, iron and folate.

OILS

It's well worth investing in a good quality extra virgin olive oil, preferably estate bottled. Keep a light olive oil for mixing with nut oils.

The most useful nut oils are hazelnut and walnut oil – try and find unrefined versions (good healthfood shops sell them) as they have a much better flavour. If you can possibly afford it invest in what I call Rolls-Royce oils, such as pistachio, pine nut or pumpkin seed oil. A few drops can lift a salad into the realms of gastronomic euphoria!

Sunflower and safflower oils are useful neutral oils which can also be mixed with nut oils. Again, the unrefined versions are infinitely superior and, on their own, are almost as good as extra virgin olive oil. Unrefined roasted groundnut (peanut) oil is another oil worth trying – it has a rich, nutty flavour.

Light sesame oil is a mild, unassertive all-purpose oil, but go easy on dark toasted sesame oil. It is very strong and should be treated more as a flavouring agent than a dressing.

VINEGARS

As with oils there are numerous vinegars from which to choose. With the exception of cider vinegar, they are made from fermented wine. The best are matured in wooden casks before bottling. It is worth paying extra for good quality vinegar.

White wine vinegar is made from any variety of white wine. It is lighter than red wine vinegar and goes best with mild-tasting leaves. Red wine vinegar is more robust and combines well with balsamic vinegar.

Balsamic vinegar is a highly aromatic vinegar made in Italy from sweet wine. It is very gutsy and a little goes a long way. Sherry vinegar is a full-bodied mellow vinegar from Spain. It goes very well with nut oils.

Rice vinegar is good for oriental-style salads and works well with sesame oil. The Japanese variety is more delicate than the Chinese.

HERBS

Fresh herbs are infinitely preferable to dried in salad making. However, dried oregano and thyme are the two exceptions. Both benefit from dry-frying to bring out the aroma. Simply put the required amount in a small heavy-based pan without any oil. Heat gently, stirring, until they begin to smell fragrant.

The supermarkets now sell a good variety of fresh herbs but it's worth growing your own, even in a pot, as there are many neglected varieties, such as lovage and savory, with magical flavours.

If, as I do, you use massive amounts of fresh coriander, chives and flat-leafed parsley, growing your own will save time and money. Otherwise, buy these herbs from ethnic shops where they are sold in sensibly sized large bunches.

I have used flat-leafed parsley in preference to the curly type. It has a different and stronger flavour and the texture seems to be more pleasing in salads.

SPICES

As with dried herbs, spices benefit from dry-frying to bring out their flavour. Spices quickly lose their flavour, so buy them in small quantities and store in a cool, dark place. Better still, buy spices whole and grind them as you need them.

SALT AND PEPPER

Always use freshly ground pepper. I think coarsely ground peppercorns look more attractive on a salad than finely ground, which can look like dust. For preference, use unground coarse sea salt flakes. They taste quite different from ordinary table salt and provide crunchy little bursts of flavour.

LEMONS AND LIMES

Lemons and limes are essential for salads. They can be interchanged but limes do have a very special warm flavour which I find quite irresistible. I use a lot of zest, meaning the thin aromatic outer layer rather than the peel. Unless you're willing to pay extra for unwaxed fruit, briefly soak them in hot water and scrub with a brush to remove the wax. Of course you will lose some of the essential oils if you do so but there seems to be no avoiding it.

MUSHROOMS

With their exotic shapes and rich flavours, mushrooms add 'meat' to main meal salads. The very best are those that you have picked yourself, as long as you are sure you have identified them correctly. Failing this, there is a good variety of cultivated mushrooms available in the supermarkets.

For using raw, I prefer organic chestnut mushrooms rather than bland button mushrooms. With their dark skins and creamy flesh they look beautiful thinly sliced. For stir-frying, try shiitake, oyster or the large flat cap variety cut into chunks. They give off delicious juices which can be added to the dressing.

SPROUTED BEANS AND SEEDS

These are the ultimate health food – easy to grow, brimful of nutrients and free from pesticides. They add a fresh-tasting flavour to salads. You can sprout almost any kind of bean or seed. Wheat sprouts are particularly sweet and delicious, fenugreek sprouts are pungent and spicy, and aduki beans have a nutty flavour. They will keep for a day or two in the fridge. If you buy them from a supermarket it's best to wash and soak them before use.

NUTS

Although I have given quantities for the shelled weight, in an ideal world nuts should be cracked just before use as they quickly go rancid. Buy them in small quantities and store them in an airtight container in a cool place.

The flavour of nuts is much richer if you dry-roast them first.

Place in a single layer in a roasting tin for 3–10 minutes, depending on the type, in a preheated oven at 180°C/350°F/gas 4. Stir them occasionally until they become golden and smell toasty.

SEEDS

Pumpkin, sesame and sunflower seeds add crunch and vitamins to salads. As with dried herbs, they benefit from dry-frying to bring out the flavour. Prepare a batch at a time and keep them in a sealed container.

SOY SAUCE

I prefer to use the traditionally made Japanese soy sauce such as shoyu or tamari (wheat-free). It has a warm, mellow flavour and is not as assertive as Chinese soy sauce. You can buy it in good healthfood stores.

EGGS

Hard-boiled eggs are an often-used ingredient in main meal salads. Simple though it may sound, boiling an egg perfectly means checking out some basics. Use large eggs (size 2). Put them in a pan and cover with cold water. Bring to the boil and simmer for exactly 4 minutes. The yolk and white will be firmly set but the centre of the yolk will still be tender. Plunge them in cold running water to stop the cooking. Shell them just before use, as the shell prevents the white drying out.

Index

amino acids, xi

apples: pickled herring, celery and apple salad, 60; smoked cheese, apple, chicory and watercress salad, 121

artichokes: salad of warm tuna, mixed beans and artichokes, 46–7; scallop and artichoke salad, 39

asparagus: asparagus, mushroom and fennel salad, 2–3; smoked salmon, prawn, asparagus and watercress salad, 63

aubergines: aubergine, chilli and sesame dip, 172; aubergine, red pepper and water chestnut salad, 28–9; dry-cured ham and aubergine salad, 84; goat's cheese and broad bean salad with, 116; oven-dried aubergines, 177; pasta, aubergine and rocket salad, 150; salad of goat's cheese, grilled aubergines and courgettes, 112–13

avocados: avocado and smoked tofu dip, 173; avocado, red onion and roasted pepper salad, 27; Californian salad platter, 29; chicken and avocado salad, 70–1; conchiglie, green bean and avocado salad, 152; guacamole, 174; kidney bean and avocado salad with two sauces, 130–1; prawn and avocado salad, 34–5; smoked salmon, pink grapefruit and avocado salad, 62; tomato and avocado salsa, 170

bacon: chicken liver, bacon and mangetout salad, 78–9; chicken wing, bacon and mushroom salad, 76–7; warm pigeon salad with, 82–3

balsamic vinaigrette, 187

Barbary duck breast, wild rice and Brazil nut salad, 80

batavia, 207

beans: salad of warm tuna, mixed beans and artichokes, 46–7; *see also* sprouted beans

beef: air-dried beef salad, 93; marinated beef salad, 92

beet greens, 207

beetroot: beetroot, orange and rocket salad, 12–13; goat's cheese, beetroot, rocket and mint salad, 110; red red salad, 14; roasted beetroot, red pepper and garlic salad, 158; smoked mackerel, beetroot and peanut salad, 59

black beans: black and white bean salad, 128; black bean, palm heart and pan-smoked sweetcorn salad, 124–5; chillied black bean salad, 123

blue cheese *see* cheese

borlotti beans: salad of pink and green beans, 126–7

215

mangetout: chicken liver, bacon and
mangetout salad, 78–9; warm pigeon
salad with, 82–3
mayonnaise: celeriac remoulade, 164;
prawn and avocado salad with garlic
mayonnaise, 34–5
meat and poultry salads, 66–100
Mediterranean fish salad, 53
Mexican cheese salad, 104
Middle Eastern salad platter, 11
mixed seafood salad with Oriental
noodles, 42–3
monkfish: Mediterranean fish salad, 53
mullet *see* red mullet
mushrooms, 212; air-dried beef salad
with salsify and, 93; asparagus,
mushroom and fennel salad with
hazelnuts, 2–3; chicken wing, bacon
and mushroom salad, 76–7;
mushroom and broad bean salad,
22–3; mushroom and coriander
salad, 162; warm salad of grilled
mushrooms, red pepper and rocket,
24–5
mustard greens, 208
mustard vinaigrette, 189

noodles, 205; Chinese chicken salad
with crispy rice noodles, 68–9;
mixed seafood salad with Oriental
noodles, 42–3; Oriental squid salad
with, 40–1
nuts, 204, 212–13

oils, xii–xiii, 204, 209–10
onions: avocado, red onion and roasted
pepper salad, 27; caramelised onion
rings, 175; salad of Italian cured
meats, tomato, onion confit and
grilled polenta, 91; spicy lamb salad
with caramelised onion rings, 96–7;
tomato-flavoured red onion confit,
176; warm goat's cheese salad with
onion confit and fennel, 114–15
oranges: beetroot, orange and rocket

salad, 12–13; blue cheese, radicchio,
orange and fennel salad, 107; carrot,
orange and ginger salad, 160; orange
and ginger vinaigrette, 193; orange
vinaigrette, 192; walnut citrus
dressing, 195
Oriental prawn salad, 33
Oriental rice and mixed vegetable salad,
149
Oriental squid salad, 40–1
Oriental vinaigrette, 189

palm hearts: black bean, palm heart and
pan-smoked sweetcorn salad, 124–5;
grilled prawn salad with, 36–7
papaya: Californian salad platter, 29;
quinoa salad with cucumber,
almonds and, 132–3; turkey and
papaya salad, 81
Parma ham and fennel salad, 87
pasta: conchiglie, green bean and
avocado salad, 152; pasta, aubergine
and rocket salad, 150; pasta,
courgette and rosemary salad, 153;
pasta salad with cheese and salami,
151
pastrami and herbed new potato salad,
89
peanuts: gado-gado, 31; Indonesian
peanut dressing, 202; quinoa salad
with bean sprouts, cucumber, chilli
and, 134–5; smoked mackerel,
beetroot and peanut salad, 59
pears: pecorino, pear, celery and
watercress salad, 120; Wensleydale,
pear and green bean salad, 103
peppercorns, 211; walnut and green
peppercorn dressing, 196
peppers: aubergine, red pepper and
water chestnut salad, 28–9; avocado,
red onion and roasted pepper salad,
27; chargrilled smoked mackerel, red
pepper and celeriac salad, 58;
chick-pea, spinach and roasted
pepper salad, 142; chillied black bean